Universals of
Second Language Acquisition

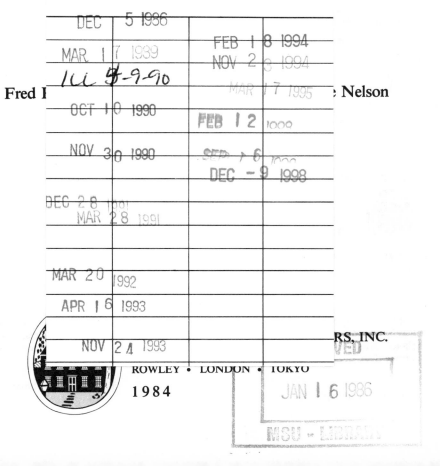

Date Due

Fred R.   Nelson

RS, INC.

ROWLEY • LONDON • TOKYO

1984

Library of Congress Cataloging in Publication Data
Main entry under title:

Universals of second language acquisition.

  Bibliography: p.
  1. Language acquisition. 2. Universals (Linguistics)
3. Interlanguage (Language learning) I. Eckman,
Fred R. II. Bell, Lawrence H. III. Nelson, Diane.
P118.U56   1984   401'.9   83-17273
ISBN 0-88377-340-6

Cover design by Leslie Bartlett.

NEWBURY HOUSE PUBLISHERS, INC.

Language Science
Language Teaching
Language Learning

ROWLEY, MASSACHUSETTS 01969
ROWLEY • LONDON • TOKYO

First printing: February 1984
5   4   3   2

Printed in the U.S.A.

To
Ellen, Leo, and Mark Eckman
Betty Bell and the memory of Richard Bell
Rita Meyers and the memory of Robert Meyers

Acknowledgments

The symposium of which this volume is the direct result was made possible by grants from the following sources:

> University of Wisconsin—Milwaukee:
>> The Department of Linguistics
>> The College of Letters and Science
>> The Division of Urban Outreach
>> The English as a Second Language Intensive Program
>> The Center for Latin America
>> The Midwest National Origin Desegregation Assistance Center

From all these units, we gratefully acknowledge support.

We would like to thank our colleagues in the Department of Linguistics, who gave freely of their time, energy, and ideas in making the symposium a success: Kathy Allen, Louise Calderone, Mary Ellis, Ashley Hastings, Gary Krukar, Edith Moravcsik, Bernice Rothenberg, Linda Rousos, Rita Rutkowski, Jody Stern, Barbara Wheatley, Martin Wininger, Jessica Wirth.

To Elizabeth Lantz and Perry McIntosh of Newbury House Publishers, we extend our appreciation for invaluable assistance and support during the editing of this volume.

Finally, but certainly not leastly, we wish to express our gratitude to Clare Brhel, Dorine Damm, and Carol Dumond for their assistance with compiling, editing, and typing the bibliography.

Contents

Introduction

On March 19 and 20, 1982, a symposium on the theme of Universals of Second Language Acquisition was held on the campus of the University of Wisconsin—Milwaukee. This symposium was attended by approximately two hundred people, and was a forum at which twenty papers were presented. The present volume is the direct result of this symposium.

The topic of universals of second language acquisition (SLA) is one which could have been raised only within the last ten or fifteen years. Prior to that, the process of SLA was generally viewed as one which involved mainly positive and negative transfer from the native language (NL) to the target language (TL). Within this context, the notion of universals could not be raised in any interesting or substantive way. Before this notion could be considered, it was necessary for the field of SLA to evolve several ideas and constructs within which the requisite empirical investigations could be carried out.

Perhaps one of the most important ideas to come forth in this context is the notion that many learner errors in SLA are not simply due to transfer (Corder 1967, Richards 1971). This opened the possibility that the learner was actually contributing something of substance to the acquisition process, and that SLA was not inextricably controlled by the NL (Dulay and Burt 1974 and elsewhere). This hypothesis is closely allied with the construct of a learner language, or interlanguage (IL) (Selinker 1972), which is a system of rules constructed by the learner for the purpose of speaking and understanding utterances in the TL. Such systems are reminiscent of the intermediate grammars constructed by children during the process of first language acquisition, though there are, of course, fundamental differences.

Armed with the hypothesis that SLA can be adequately explained only be postulating interlanguages, researchers in the field could raise the issue of whether in fact it was necessary to distinguish between first and second language acquisition, or whether one could speak of a single acquisition process (Taylor 1974). One problem in not distinguishing first and second language acquisition was the fact that, while first language acquisition almost always proceeds to completion, SLA rarely does. Rather, the second language learner typically reaches a point where the acquisition has ceased, but the learner's speech is characterized by "accent" or by imperfect learning. One of the ways in which researchers have sought to explain this difference between first and second language acquisition is by appealing to some of the differences in the context in which SLA takes place, as opposed to that in which first languages are acquired (Gardner and Lambert 1972, Taylor 1974).

Now, given that the concept of interlanguage facilitates raising the question of whether first and second language acquisition are similar, the purported similarity of the two acquisition processes enables one to consider the prospect that there may be universals of SLA, perhaps similar to those that have been proposed for first language acquisition (FLA). Before considering this question in more detail, it would be worthwhile to look at the role that universals have played in at least some approaches to FLA.

Within this context, the question that surrounds any proposed universal of language is why this particular aspect or phenomenon of language is universal. Few, if any, good explanations have been advanced as an answer to this question. Rather, it has generally been assumed that universals are innate (Chomsky 1966); they are assumed to provide the principles of organization that make language learning possible. Consequently, universals do not have to be learned by the language learner because they inhere in the basic cognitive ability that all humans possess in order to acquire their ambient language(s), and it is for this reason that any given universal is common to all languages (Chomsky 1966). From this viewpoint it is clear that the study of universals is closely allied with the study of the principles involved in FLA.

This being the case, universals have generally been dichotomized into two major types: formal and substantive (Chomsky 1965). Formal universals refer to the form that a grammar of any language must take and to the abstract conditions that such grammars must meet. Put somewhat differently, formal universals help to specify a theory of possible grammars, or in other words, they help to determine a metatheory or what Chomsky (1965) has called a general linguistic theory. Substantive universals, on the other hand, pertain to statements that are empirical generalizations about the forms or representations, such as phones, phonemes, morphemes, lexical items, and sentence types, that make up the set of human languages. Substantive universals, then, are less abstract and less theory-dependent than formal universals.

To take some concrete examples, a proposed formal universal is the notion that a grammar consists of a set of phrase structure rules and lexicon, which define a level of deep structure; another is the constraint that cyclic rules apply from the most-included to the least-included domain of a rule. An example of a substantive universal is the statement that all languages which have aspirated voiced stops also have unaspirated voiced stops, but the reverse is not true. Another substantive universal is that all languages in which the basic order of elements has verbs following their respective objects also have auxiliaries following their respective verbs.

Looked at in the light of second language acquisition, universals of SLA can be seen to play the same role as in the study of FLA. More specifically, universals of SLA limit the possible variation in interlanguages. This limited variation may be due in part to the fact that the NL and TL involved obey certain universal constraints and therefore do not vary infinitely and randomly. In addition, universals of SLA may also be indicative of universal learning strategies (Dulay and Burt 1974), or equivalently, Chomky's (1966) principles of organization. Thus, the roles that universals play in the study of SLA can be viewed as being analogous to that played by universals in studying FLA.

Continuing this analogy, it is possible to formulate a set of principles governing the types of rules (grammars) which are motivated for ILs. That is, one can formulate a metatheory for interlanguages. Likewise, it is possible to investigate ILs for the purpose of determining whether there are any empirical generalizations which can be maintained for all interlanguages.

Along these lines, the papers in this volume fall generally into three main categories: (1) the development of metatheory about interlanguages, as well as proposing a theory about how second languages are acquired; (2) affective variables involved in the acquisition and use of second languages; and (3) empirical studies on interlanguages. The papers in this third area have been grouped further into two subsections: those dealing with the comparison of first and second language acquisition, and those dealing exclusively with universal aspects of SLA.

The papers which focus on the theoretical and metatheoretical aspects of interlanguages and SLA in general are those by Tarone, Stevick, and Seliger. Tarone's paper deals with the comparison and evaluation of three paradigms, or metatheories, in terms of accounting for interlanguage variability. After documenting the variation inherent in ILs, Tarone makes explicit some of the assumptions which each paradigm makes concerning the learner's knowledge of his or her IL, the principles which underlie a learner's language behavior, the data which have a bearing on testing hypotheses about ILs, and the explanation for the observed IL variability. She argues for the superiority of one of the paradigms over the other two on the basis of its ability to better explain the variability associated with interlanguages.

Stevick's paper addresses the distinction which is often made in SLA literature between *learning* and *acquisition*. He argues for the fundamental unity of these two processes and concludes that they are at the opposite ends of a continuum. According to Stevick, learning and acquisition correlate, respectively, with what he terms *poorly integrated* and *well-integrated* contexts. Despite the negative and positive connotations that are associated with these respective terms, Stevick goes on to point out that learning and acquisition both have a positive role to play in language teaching. Whereas acquisition produces a result in which the language is more readily usable for communicative purposes, learning often results in a situation where the form of the learned word or pattern is clear.

Seliger proposes a model of language acquisition which addresses a number of paradoxes surrounding the second language acquisition researcher, and which attempts to account for the fact that virtually every human language is learnable, to at least some extent, by virtually all human beings. Seliger's model postulates two levels of processing. The first, called *strategy*, is an innate, learner-independent process of hypothesis formation and testing. The other, termed *tactic*, is learner- and context-dependent and is much less predictable than the level of strategy. The interface between these two levels is provided by a *learner's filter*. It is this filter which accounts for some of the individual differences in SLA, despite the postulation of universal strategies.

Thus, the three papers in this section address the topic of SLA from three different directions. Tarone approaches the problem of interlanguage variability, Stevick takes up the question of SLA in terms of situational context, and Seliger directs his attention to individual and functional variation in interlanguage.

The next section of the book contains two papers dealing with affective aspects of SLA and with communicative competence. The first paper in this section, that by Kaplan and Shand, is a study which tests the hypothesis that learners with a strong integrative motivation ("+I learners") will tend to acquire those aspects of the TL which are related more to the meaning of an utterance than to the form. Specifically, such learners will, according to the hypothesis, have a greater concern with communicating with members of the target culture than with correct grammar. The authors point out that a reasonable opposing hypothesis would be that +I learners will want to speak and write as much like native speakers as possible and therefore will attend to grammatical form along with meaning.

The paper by Saville-Troike, McClure, and Fritz is an ethnography of the acquisition of English by 20 children, ranging in age from 7 to 12 years, who were enrolled in a multilingual program in the Urbana, Illinois, public school system. This study addresses the question of what these children need to accomplish in various communicative contexts, and what tactics they use, both verbally and nonverbally, to do this. Using the system for coding speech acts developed by Dore (1978) and extending it to include nonverbal acts, the authors found that there was an apparent universality of tactics for conversations, and that there were two basic tactics used for narratives. The authors also report one counterexample to a universal proposed by Wong-Fillmore (1976), namely, that social contact is critical in second language development. In this study, some children who were not sociable were among those who acquired the most in terms of English vocabulary and grammar.

The third section of this volume contains papers which report on empirical studies of interlanguages and which fall into two general subcategories: those which compare the process of SLA with first language acquisition and those which deal only with SLA.

Flynn's paper is an experimental study which addresses the question of whether primary branching direction (PBD) is a factor in SLA. After defining PBD, Flynn cites work on first language acquisition which shows that PBD is a principle which provides a significant constraint on children's early language development. Thus, she hypothesizes that SLA will be superior when there is a match between the NL and TL in PBD as opposed to when there is a mismatch. Moreover, there will be differences in the processing of complex sentences during early stages of SLA when the TL and NL match versus when they do not match. To test these hypotheses, Flynn obtained data from two different NL groups: Spanish, which has the same PBD as English, and Japanese, which has a different PBD. The results confirmed the hypotheses and showed PBD to be a significant principle of SLA.

VanPatten's paper deals with what has been termed the "natural sequence" (Dulay and Burt 1974) in the acquisition of certain English morphemes by children who speak other languages. Bailey, Madden, and Krashen (1974) define an order of difficulty for the same set of morphemes for adult learners of English. VanPatten shows that, if the morphemes are considered in terms of the lexical category to which they are affixed, one can reconcile any differences in the acquisition of these morphemes among child first language learners, child second language learners, and adult second language learners. In view of this, VanPatten goes on to consider whether there is no substantive difference between first and second language acquisition, and offers an explanation for why the orders of acquisition are the same.

The second subgroup of this section begins with a study by Adjémian and Liceras which examines the interaction of three factors, namely, universal grammar, attained linguistic knowledge and metalinguistic abilities in the acquisition of restrictive relative clauses by adults. Three target languages were dealt with: English, French, and Spanish; and data were gathered in both oral and written modes, using several different tasks. The authors found that the acquisition of some subtle differences in relative clauses across languages had no straightforward explanation. Rather, the emerging IL is shaped by a number of factors, including universal grammar, transfer, and learner-specific hypotheses.

Mazurkewich takes up the issue of markedness with respect to the acquisition of dative questions. Her hypothesis for this study was that the unmarked form of the dative question, the one with the preposition moved with the wh-word, would be acquired before the marked form, the one with the preposition "stranded," despite the fact that the unmarked form probably occurs quite infrequently in the learner's input. The subjects for the study were a group of Inuktitut speakers and another of French speakers, both of whom were learning English. The data were gathered by means of using a written, operational test, and support the hypotheses that the unmarked form is acquired prior to the marked form.

The paper by Kumpf is a study of the tense-aspectual system of the interlanguage of a native speaker of Japanese who had learned English in a natural, untutored context. After arguing that the discourse, rather than the sentence, is the proper domain of study, Kumpf presents data to illustrate various facts about verbs in the subject's interlanguage. From this, she concludes that completed action in the foreground of the discourse is expressed with an unmarked, nontensed form of the verb, and that, in the background, many verbs, especially those that are stative, are tensed. This system which the speaker has created, Kumpf points out, is like neither the NL nor the TL, and corresponds closely to tense-aspectual systems found in other languages such as Yoruba and Igbo. Thus, the tense-aspect system of Kumpf's subject conforms to certain universals, or universal tendencies, in languages of the world.

In short, the papers in this volume deal with those same properties of SLA and interlanguages as previous studies have with respect to first language acquisition and primary languages. Thus, it is possible to consider theoretical as well as metatheoretical aspects of interlanguages, to write descriptions of these interlanguage systems, and to study the context in which second languages are used and learned. Moreover, and this is the crux of the whole volume, it is possible to consider all these properties with a view toward universals.

Universals of
Second Language Acquisition

PART I

Theories of
Second Language Acquisition

1 On the Variability of Interlanguage Systems[1]

Elaine Tarone
University of Minnesota

One phenomenon which must be accounted for by any theory of second language acquisition is the phenomenon of systematic variability in the utterances produced by second language learners as they attempt to communicate in the target language. Learner utterances have been shown to be systematically variable in at least two senses. First, *linguistic context* may have a variable effect on the learner's use of related phonological and syntactic structures (see Hyltenstam 1977,1978; Dickerson 1974; Dickerson and Dickerson 1977). Second, the *task* used for the elicitation of data from learners may have a variable effect on the learner's production of related phonological and syntactic structures. It is this second type of variation which I would like to consider in this paper, because it raises a number of interesting problems for a theory of interlanguage (IL).

In this paper, I will present data from several studies showing that IL speech production[2] varies systematically with elicitation task, I will compare the fundamental assumptions of three paradigms for the study of interlanguage, and I will show that one of these paradigms accounts for the data better than the other two.

DATA ON IL VARIABILITY

The variation of IL syntax, morphology, and phonology due to the influence of elicitation task has been well documented.

In *syntax,* for example, Schmidt (1980) found that learners from several native language (NL) backgrounds varied in their treatment of a rule allowing second-verb ellipsis in English, as in 1:

1   Mary is eating an apple and Sue Ø a pear.

In Table 1, we see that these learners *never* produced a sentence like 1 in free oral production. When asked to repeat such a sentence a few seconds after a native speaker of English in an elicited imitation task, 11 percent could do so (most supplied the missing second verb). When asked to combine two sentences

3

Table 1.   Variable Second-Verb Deletion in Four Elicitation Tasks for Nine Learners of English L2

	Free oral production	Elicited imitation	Written sentence— combining	Grammatical judgment
1. Mary is eating an apple and Sue Ø a pear	0%	11%	25%	50%

From data in Schmidt (1980).

with identical verbs, 25 percent deleted the second verb. And, when asked to say whether sentences like 1 were grammatical in English, 50 percent said they were. So these four different elicitation tasks seem to provide us with four different pictures of the status of this rule in the ILs of these subjects; this variability is systematic, with sentences like 1 increasing gradually from more casual free speech to more careful grammatical judgments. (Further evidence that IL syntax varies with task is provided by LoCoco 1976.)

In Table 2, we see that a similar pattern exists in an example of IL *morphology*. Fairbanks (1982) found that a Japanese learner of English almost never used the third-person singular -s morpheme in casual speech, producing utterances 2 to 4 and others like them:

2   *. . . if she *have* a ch-children . . .
3   *Because she *have* to care their son . . .
4   *He *live* with their ch . . .

However, in his careful style, this speaker almost always supplied the morpheme—for singular *and* plural verbs:

5   . . . each store uh *has* er own price.
6   That store uh *sells* uh this transportation.
7   Um some uh station *says* uh Minneapolis . . .
8   *Some parts of town uh *has* a lots of food and others *has* a lots of medicine.
9   *What *mean* we grown up together?

Such style shifting in IL morphology is not unusual. Krashen (1981) and others have shown in cross-sectional studies that elicitation tasks which give the learner more time produce different morpheme rank orders than tasks which do

Table 2.   Variable Production of Third Person Singular -s Morpheme by a Japanese Speaker of English L2

Casual style	Careful style
2. *. . . if she *have* a ch-children . . .	5. . . . each store uh *has* er own price
3. *Because she *have* to care their son . . .	6. That store uh *sells* uh this transportation
4. *He *live* with their ch . . .	7. Um some uh station *says* uh Minneapolis . . .
	8. *Some parts of town uh *has* a lots of food and others *has* a lots of medicine.
	9. *What *mean* we grown up together?

From data in Fairbanks (1982).

not. [For example, Larsen-Freeman (1975) found that rank orders of morphemes produced by second language learners varied across five tasks of "speaking, listening, reading, writing and elicited imitation." When rank orders on one task were compared with orders on another task, "few statistically significant correlations were found" (p. 416). Krashen (1976) suggested that elicitation tasks which gave the learner more time and focused on form, not communication, produced morpheme rank orders in which the third person singular morpheme and the regular past morpheme were more accurately produced than in other tasks, as these morphemes are more easily "learned" consciously.]

Table 3 shows that IL *phonology* is also systematically variable. Dickerson and Dickerson (1977) found that Japanese learners of English produced /r/ with varying degrees of correctness, depending on whether they were speaking freely, reading a dialogue, or reading a word list. Correct production of target language (TL) /r/ occurred most frequently in careful speech and least frequently in casual speech.

Thus far, we have seen that systematic variability is associated with elicitation task on the levels of syntax, morphology, and phonology. Further, it seems that the pattern is for the TL variant to be supplied more frequently in the careful styles elicited by some tasks, and less frequently in the casual styles of IL elicited by other tasks.

The picture in Table 4 is more complicated. Here, the TL variant [Θ] which occurs in the more careful IL style (elicited in a minimal pair task) is also a

Table 3.   Correct Production of /r/ in Contexts: C/r/mid-vowel and C/r/high vowel

Dickerson and Dickerson (1977).

Table 4.   Realizations of the TH-variable in Arabic (L1) and English (IL) by All Subjects

	Reading passage	Word list	Minimal pairs
Interdental pronunciations, Arabic (L1)	33%	64%	77%
Θ as opposed to *t, s,* English (IL)	54%	73%	73%

From Schmidt (1977).

Table 5.   Number and Percentage of Tokens for Each IL Variant
of the R Variable in Two Different Speech Styles of Thais Learning
English (L2)

| | Speech style | | | |
| | Conversation | | Listing | |
IL variant	No.	%	No.	%
Initial R				
TL variant (correct)				
ɹ	30	38.5	4	8.9
New variants				
ɹʴ	40	51.3	5	11.1
ɻ	2	2.6		
ɹ̞	3	3.8	15	33.3
w̃ɹʴ			1	2.2
ɹ			2	4.4
ɭ			1	2.2
NL variants (interference)				
ɪ̈			3	6.7
ř	3	3.8	3	6.7
r̃			11	24.4
Totals	78	100	45	99.9
Final R				
TL variants (correct)				
ɹ	9	4.6		
ɹʴ	72	36.5	13	72.2
Possible NL interference				
∅	65	33	3	16.7
ə	49	24.9	2	11.1
New variant				
w	2	1.1		
Totals	197	100.1	18	100

Beebe (1980).

prestige variant of the NL, Arabic, and occurs in the more careful NL style. In this case, the same kind of style shifting seems to occur when the learners perform the same three tasks in their NL and in their IL. We could even say that a sociolinguistic rule is transferred from the NL into the IL here. Here, the [Θ] of the careful IL style may be both the TL [Θ] (as in Table 3) and the NL prestige [Θ]. We will return to Table 4 shortly.

Table 5 provides more detailed information on the kinds of structures which may occur in the IL careful style. Here we see that Thai learners of English supply /r/ variably, depending on whether they are conversing or listing words. We see that in producing *final* /r/ in IL, the learners follow the general pattern we have noted, supplying more TL variants in the careful style (listing words) than in the casual (conversing): /r/ is 36.5 percent correct in the casual style and 72.2 percent correct in the careful style. But in producing *initial* /r/ in IL, the learners violate the general pattern we have noted; they produce *fewer* TL

Table 5 (continued)

Key to IL phonetic variants of R:

ɹ	= a retroflex continuant; considered correct (native) in initial or final position in American English; not native to Thai.
ɹˈ	= a more open, less retroflex, continuant; considered correct (native New York English) in final position but incorrect initially; not native to Thai.
ɻ̥	= a voiceless retroflex continuant; IL variant in initial position.
ɹ̰	= a retroflex, postalveolar fricative; IL variant initial position.
wɹˈ	= an /ɹˈ/ preceded by English labio-velar continuant; initial position IL variable.
r	= a rolled fricative; IL variant in initial position.
ɭ	= a retroflex, postalveolar lateral; IL variant in initial position.
!	= an apico-alveolar or denti-alveolar clear lateral with flaplike quality due to tense articulation and sudden release; initial IL variant borrowed from Thai.
ř	= an apico-alveolar flap; initial position IL variant transferred from Thai.
r̃	= an apico-alveolar trill; initial position IL variant transferred from Thai.
∅	= zero sound for postvocalic R; final position IL variant either transferred from Thai or acquired from "r-less" dialect of English.
ə	= mid-central vowel; final position IL variant either transferred from Thai or acquired from "r-less" dialect of English.
w	= labio-velar continuant; final position IL variant.

variants (8.9 percent) in their careful style and *more* (38.5 percent) in their casual IL style. Furthermore, their careful style seems to be marked by more *native* language variants than the casual. It turns out that these NL variants are prestige variants of initial /r/ which are used more frequently in careful styles in Thai; the learners are using prestige NL variants to an increasing degree in their IL careful style. This may also be the process followed by the Arabic learners in Table 4—a process obscured by the fact that their prestige NL variant also *happens* to be the target variant in English.

The data we have examined thus far indicate that the IL *careful* style (elicited by tasks like grammatical judgments, word list reading, and sentence combining) may be characterized (1) sometimes by more TL variants than the casual style, and (2) sometimes by more NL prestige variants than the casual style (elicited in conversation).

Table 6 contains data on IL syntax which provide some information on the kinds of structures which may occur in the IL *casual* style. Felix (1980) found that German learners of English when repeating drills in a formal classroom consistently produced correct English (TL) negation. Their teachers always produced correct English negative patterns. However, on those few occasions

Table 6. Spontaneous Productions by German (L1) Learners of English in First Three Weeks of Formal Classroom Exposure: Negation and Yes/No Question Inversion

10. It's no my comb.
11. Britta no this . . . no have . . . this . . .

From Felix (1980).

when the learners were allowed to use English in conversation for meaningful communication, they produced these utterances:

10	It's no my comb.
11	Britta no this . . . no have . . . this . . .

Sentences 10 and 11 cannot be traced to either the NL or the TL. These patterns do not occur in German, and the students had never heard these structures in English. These structures, produced in the learners' less careful speech style, seem to be similar to simple structures which occur in many pidgin languages, in early child language acquisition, and in early untutored second language acquisition. We might view such simple structures as evidencing acquisitional universals. Such structures seem to be used spontaneously by these learners in their more casual speech style.

Thus, the data we have examined thus far indicate that interlanguage does vary systematically with elicitation task and, further, that when a task elicits a relatively more careful style, that style may contain more TL variants or more prestige NL variants than the relatively more casual style elicited by other tasks. The more casual style may contain structures traceable to neither the NL nor the TL, structures which arise spontaneously in the casual style and resemble structures which occur in pidgins, in early child language acquisition, and in early untutored second language acquisition.

THREE PARADIGMS FOR THE STUDY OF INTERLANGUAGE

The type of IL variability we have just seen is problematic for a theory of interlanguage because it raises the issue of whether or not a second language learner's language is *systematic,* and if so, how. Interlanguage was originally defined by Selinker (1972) as a "separate linguistic *system*" which was hypothesized to underlie "a learner's attempted production of a TL [target language] norm" (p. 214). Selinker explicitly rejected the use of certain kinds of elicitation tasks in obtaining data for the study of interlanguage. Specifically, he argued that the "only observable data to which we can relate predictions" in a theory of second language learning are "the utterances which are produced when the learner attempts to say sentences of a TL." Thus, Selinker explicitly rejected the use, for example, of a learner's grammatical intuitions about his IL, because these would only "provide information about another system, the one the learner is struggling with, i.e., the TL."[3]

Since Selinker's proposal, of course, as we have seen, researchers *have* used a variety of elicitation tasks, following Corder (1973). In fact, Schachter, Tyson, and Diffley (1976) take the opposite position from Selinker, arguing that grammatical intuitions *must* be used to characterize interlanguage:

> We believe that NO attempt at the characterization of the learner's interlanguage which is based solely on collecting and organizing the utterances produced by the learner will be descriptively adequate (Chomsky 1965). We are interested in characterizing learner *knowledge* of his language, not simply learner production (p. 67).

One question we now have is, given that we have seen that different elicitation tasks produce variation in the second language learner's speech production, so that use of one or another task may lead to contradictory claims about the structure of interlanguage, what are the best data to use to characterize IL? Even more fundamentally, what kind of system is it which can be hypothesized to underlie learner utterances, given the variation in the data?

At present, at least three paradigms for the study of interlanguage seem to be emerging, each with a distinctly different conception of the nature of the IL system, the nature of variation in IL, and the best data to be used in studying IL. These are:

1. The homogeneous competence paradigm, as described by Adjémian (1976, 1982), which applies a Chomskian paradigm for the study of language to the interlanguage situation
2. The capability continuum paradigm, as described by Tarone (1979, 1982), which views IL as consisting of a continuum of styles
3. The dual knowledge paradigm, as described by Krashen (1981 and elsewhere), which is part of the monitor theory.

In this section, I will examine some of the assumptions which underlie each of these three paradigms, and will contrast them. In the process, I will evaluate the paradigms in terms of how well they account for the data we have just (briefly) examined, and conclude that paradigm 2 accounts for those data best. A simplified outline of the assumptions of the three paradigms is provided in the appendix.

In the following discussion, I presuppose that the immediate goal of research in the field of second language acquisition is the description of learners' underlying grammatical and phonological capabilities (their interlanguage). I assume that in meeting this goal, linguists have the aim of writing a model of the underlying linguistic capabilities of the individual learner.[4] Each individual's linguistic capabilities are changing over time, so that the linguist must in fact write a succession of models to account for the learner's changing IL over time. I assume that examination of several such models of individual learner ILs will show that they share certain universal properties; no individual IL will be utterly idiosyncratic. It is clear, as Adjémian (1982) has pointed out, that this attempt to describe the learner's IL is part of a larger goal, which is to develop a theory of non-primary-language acquisition.

I believe that all three paradigms in our field share this general conception of the immediate goal of research. But they differ in their basic assumptions about the nature of the linguistic capability being modeled, and the place of variability in the model, and thus they differ in their assumptions about the best data to use in accomplishing their goal.

Paradigm 1: Homogeneous Competence

Paradigm 1 is essentially the Chomskian paradigm applied to an interlanguage situation. The first three assumptions outlined below are assumptions which hold for the study of *native* languages—the fourth assumption asserts that these all hold for the study of *interlanguages* as well.

Assumption 1: Linguistic Competence. One goal of linguists is to construct a model of the linguistic knowledge, or competence, of an idealized speaker-hearer. The speaker-hearer, in this case, is a native speaker of the language and is idealized in the sense that he is conceptualized as existing outside of any specific communicative situation, and as unaffected by such irrelevant occurrences as slips of the tongue and false starts. The speaker-hearer's sociolinguistic knowledge—the knowledge of how to use different registers in different social situations—is not relevant to the linguist's goal, which is to construct a model of the speaker-hearer's purely linguistic knowledge. This competence is assumed to be homogeneous—that is, it is the unvarying competence of an idealized single-style speaker-hearer. This competence is accessible to a form of introspection, in that the speaker-hearer may use it to make judgments of grammaticality.

Assumption 2: What Guides Language Behavior. This competence allows the native speaker to judge grammaticality of sentences and also underlies the speaker-hearer's actual performance in speaking and hearing. That is, it is assumed that the *same* competence which produces grammatical intuitions is also the competence which underlies the individual's speech production. This follows logically from assumption 1 of a homogeneous competence—a single-style speaker. In other words, the unconscious rules of a language which allow the production of utterances in that language are somehow manifested or "mirrored" [Baker's (1978) term] in a speaker/hearer's conscious judgments about that language.

Assumption 3: Linguistic Data. (a) The *best* data to use to gain access to that linguistic knowledge consist of that set of sentences which the native speaker of the language *judges* to be grammatical, or ungrammatical, or ambiguous. That is, native speaker intuitions are used to select that set of sentences which the linguist will use as data in constructing his grammar.[5]

(b) Other data, such as incidentally observed utterances or even written texts, may be added to the basic pool of data provided by intuitions. A crucial point here is that because the native speaker-hearer is assumed to have a homogeneous competence (a single style), data from these various sources *may* be (and often are) combined indiscriminately to form a single pool of data, all of which may be used in constructing a model of the speaker's "homogeneous competence."

Assumption 4: Interlanguage Competence, Data and Performance. The same goal, and the same sort of data, may be used in studying interlanguage— the linguistic system which underlies a learner's attempted utterances in the TL. The researcher elicits the learner's intuitions on grammaticality in order to obtain a body of data to be used in constructing a model of the learner's linguistic knowledge in IL—a grammar.

> Le besoin d'un modèle abstrait, idéalisé de la grammaire de l'apprenant. . . a comme corollaire la nécessité de trier soigneusement les données sur la base desquelles on élaborera notre modèle. Ces données doivent être celles produite par les intuitions grammaticales de l'apprenant (par sa connaissance implicite. . .) et non pas celles enregistrées par hasard au cours d'une entrevue, et qui resteraient non reproductibles.

> The need for an abstract model, idealized from the learner's grammar. . . has as a corollary the necessity of carefully selecting the data on the foundation of which we will elaborate our model. These data must be those produced by the grammatical intuitions of the learner (through his implicit knowledge. . .) and not those recorded by chance in the course of an interview, and which remain non-reproducible (Adjémian, Introduction).[6]

At this point, it may be worthwhile to stop and reflect on these assumptions in light of the IL data we reviewed earlier. Can the notion of the idealized homogeneous competence possibly be stretched to fit the second language learner's situation? In particular, assumption 2—that the same homogeneous competence underlies grammatical intuitions and speech production—seems incompatible with the data in Table 1, for example, where the learners' intuitions and their speech production seem quite different. Adjémian is left with the task of accounting for this variability while retaining the notion of the homogeneous competence.

Assumption 3*a*, that the best data are intuitional data, seems rather arbitrary. The intuitional IL data in Table 1 do seem to provide more evidence of TL influence than data from the other tasks given the learners. But, in what sense are these data *better* than data from casual conversation, where we may find evidence of structures truly unique to the IL—that is, traceable to neither TL nor NL? Assumption 3*b*, that one can indiscriminately pool different kinds of data in modeling competence, also seems untenable in light of the data. Can we possibly gain an accurate picture of IL competence by *pooling* the data in Table 1? If we pool it, do we give all styles the same weight? Is there a formula we can use to combine these data?

There seem to be some problems with these assumptions in light of the data.

Assumption 5: IL Variability. Adjémian says we may expect to see a difference between that set of sentences which the learner judges to be grammatical in IL, and that set of utterances which the learner himself produces. This is because, in speech production, the IL is permeable to invasion from other rule systems.

> L'apprenant produira parfois des structures qui seront agrammaticales par rapport à la grammaire de son IL. C'est-à-dire, la systématicité interne de sa grammaire-IL sera violée. Ce phénomène est dû au fait que l'IL est perméable (Adjémian 1976) et permet à des règles de la L1 de se glisser dans son système, ou permet des surgénéralisations de ses propres règles.

> The learner will, on occasion, produce structures which are ungrammatical with respect to his IL grammar. That is, the internal systematicity of his IL grammar will be violated. This phenomenon is due to the fact that IL is permeable (Adjémian 1976), permitting the rules of the L1 to creep into the system, and also permitting overgeneralization of its own (IL) rules (Adjémian 3.3).

This paradigm assumes that there will be variation between the learner's grammatical intuitions (on the basis of which his "IL grammar" is written) and some of the learner's utterances *using* the IL. Adjémian's way of maintaining the notion of homogeneous competence and also accounting for variability is to argue that the homogeneous competence is permeable to invasion from other language systems in the production of utterances. We see now that utterances are not produced by the underlying IL competence alone, but also by other grammatical systems which have invaded the IL system in performance.

The problem with this solution is that it does not adequately account for the data. The data indicate that, if anything is permeable to invasion from TL and NL, it is the *careful* style and (in Table 1) grammatical intuitions. The casual, conversational style of the learners in Table 6, on the other hand, seems to be signally impermeable to influence from the TL and NL. The data seem to show the opposite of what this paradigm would predict.

Note in summary that in Adjémian's Paradigm 1, the learner's competence is considered to be homogeneous and accessible to a kind of introspection, in that learners have grammatical intuitions which the linguist may use as data in modeling that competence. Variation is a phenomenon which occurs in speech production, because of permeability, but not in judging grammaticality. That is, permeability occurs in speech performance and not in the grammatical intuitions on the basis of which the "grammar itself" is written.

As I have pointed out, problems arise when the Chomskian theoretical framework (as expressed by Adjémian) is applied in this way to the case of second language acquisition (SLA). The case of SLA violates several assumptions which are basic to this framework. With SLA, the task is to describe and explain a grammar which is not native; which results from contact between a native language and another language, with possible constraints from universals; and which is in formation, and therefore seems to have heterogeneity built into it.[7] This linguistic paradigm's notion of the ideal speaker-hearer with a homogeneous competence, able to provide intuitions of grammaticality which lead to an understanding of that which underlies performance, seems to be antithetical to all the basic facts which characterize the second language learner's situation. Certainly the assumptions of paradigm 1 cannot account for the interlanguage data we have examined in this paper.

Paradigm 2: Capability Continuum

Paradigm 2 seems to me to account for the data best. This paradigm is presupposed in my own work (Tarone 1979,1982) and in that of Dickerson (1974) and others. This paradigm differs in important ways from the homogeneous competence paradigm just described. Perhaps most important is the difference in the way in which the two paradigms conceive of the underlying system which is being modeled, the consequent differences in their view of the nature of variability, and their different notions of the best sort of data to use in studying IL.

As I have pointed out elsewhere (Tarone 1979), this paradigm is founded on the assumption that the axioms of Labov's (1969) observer's paradox apply to interlanguage. I repeat the first three axioms, which are most relevant to our current discussion:

1. There are no single-style speakers. Every speaker shifts linguistic and phonetic variables as the situation and topic change.
2. It is possible to range the styles of a speaker along a continuous dimension defined by the amount of attention paid to speech.
3. In the vernacular style, where the minimum amount of attention is given to speech, the most regular and systematic of phonological and grammatical patterns are evidenced. Other styles tend to show more variability (Labov 1969).

We shall return to these axioms in the course of our discussion.

Assumption 1: IL Capability. The learner's IL capability is that which underlies, or guides, the regular language behavior of the second language learner. The term "capability" is used instead of the term "competence," as "competence" implies the sort of "linguistic knowledge" meant in paradigm 1, a knowledge accessible almost in its entirety to a form of introspection in that grammatical judgments may provide the linguist more or less direct access to it.

The learner's IL capability as defined in this paradigm is not assumed to be homogeneous but is assumed to be heterogeneous, as it is made up of a continuum of styles. Following Labov (1969), we may of course say that any linguistic system must be viewed as consisting of a continuum of styles. Any system—including an IL system—has its own superordinate style, which we may define as that style produced when the speaker pays the most attention to language form. It is this style which is probably modeled by the grammar of paradigm 1. In comparison, paradigm 2 views the capability of the speaker of an IL as also including a "vernacular" style, which (following Labov) we may define as that style produced when the speaker pays the least amount of attention to language form. The capability of the speaker of interlanguage includes both the superordinate and the vernacular styles of the system, and the intermediate continuum of styles which makes up the system of IL. A "grammar" may be written for each style in the continuum, and these "grammars" may be systematically related to one another in our model of the IL capability continuum. This IL is *systematic* in two senses: (1) it is describable and predictable in terms of a set of variable and categorical rules; and (2) it has internal consistency (Tarone 1982).

Paradigm 2 maintains the same distinction between underlying IL capability and IL behavior that paradigm 1 maintains between competence and performance. The underlying IL capability is an idealized linguistic system consisting of a range of styles; in speech performance a speaker may (for a variety of psychological or social reasons) choose to make use of one style or another. But the system itself is an abstract linguistic system which is inferred to exist apart from any particular instance of its use.

I will show that paradigm 2's conception of the nature of the underlying IL system will enable us to postulate a notion of variability which will help us to account for the data in Tables 1 to 6 better than paradigm 1 can.

Assumption 2: What Underlies IL Language Behavior. It is the continuum described in assumption 1 which underlies IL behavior. Following the second axiom of Labov's observer's paradox, we may say that that portion of the continuum which underlies a particular instance of regular learner performance is determined primarily by the degree of attention which the learner pays to language form in that instance. Note that it is only *regular* IL behavior which is accounted for here; slips of the tongue and irregular occurrences of language behavior are *not* to be accounted for by the underlying continuum. In Table 1, for example, that part of the continuum underlying free oral production does not allow second-verb ellipsis; a grammar modeling this part of the continuum would not contain such a rule. On the other hand, that part of the continuum underlying grammatical judgment behavior *does* allow second-verb ellipsis but does so variably; a grammar modeling this part of the continuum would contain a variable rule for second-verb ellipsis.

Note also a major difference between paradigms 1 and 2, with regard to the nature of the system actually underlying learner performance. Paradigm 1 (because of its assumptions about the nature of IL competence) is forced to assume that it is not only IL competence which underlies learner performance but also other linguistic systems (the NL, for instance, or the TL) which "invade" the learner's competence. But surely if other linguistic systems are able to "invade" in this way, they must be *known* to learners in some sense, and thus be part of their linguistic knowledge, their competence. The status of these "invading systems" vis-à-vis IL competence is unclear. Perhaps because of this, paradigm 1 does not make clear predictions about what happens when systems invade; the process does not seem to be rule-governed in any sense. Paradigm 2's solution is more elegant: there is a single systematic continuum which underlies a learner's behavior. This continuum is describable by rule in a way which the "invading systems" approach does not seem to be. Even if paradigm 1 were to add optional rules (Adjémian), it would not have the predictive power which paradigm 2 has, as we shall see. I will show later that paradigm 2's solution will, in addition to being more elegant, enable us to describe and predict the variability in the data *better* than is possible within paradigm 1.

Assumption 3: Data Used to Study IL. Observation of learner utterances when minimum attention is paid to language form will provide data about the vernacular—only one style within the range of styles which make up the learner's IL. Observation of learner utterances when maximum attention is paid to form will provide data about the superordinate style, toward the opposite end of the learner's IL continuum. Elicitation of learner judgements of grammaticality encourages the learner to pay even more attention to language form than when producing utterances; hence intuitions of grammaticality provide data on the extreme superordinate end of the continuum.[8]

Paradigm 2 demands the use of many kinds of data (ranging from tasks like reading word lists and texts, combining sentences, and elicited imitation to conversation in circumstances requiring more or less attention to language form), data which must be kept separate from one another in order to provide information about all the styles which make up the continuum of the IL system.

Assumption 4: Nature and Cause of IL Variability. That variability [9] in the regular language behavior of second language learners which is associated with the use of different elicitation tasks is caused by style shifting along the IL continuum, which in turn is caused by variable shifts in the degree of attention which the learner pays to language form (see Tarone 1982 for a discussion of the role of attention in style shifting of this kind). The various styles of the IL may be described and related to one another in terms of a set of underlying variable and categorical rules.[10] So in Table 3, the rule for /r/ production is almost categorical in reading word lists; /r/ is supplied almost 100 percent of the time. But /r/ is supplied only 50 percent of the time in free speech, where we assume that the learners are paying less attention to speech form; the rule here has become more variable in this less superordinate style.

At any one point in time, as the learner style-shifts toward an IL superordinate norm as a result of paying more attention to language form, some categorical rules may become more variable, and some variable rules may become more categorical, as they are increasingly influenced by the TL (or NL prestige norm). In Table 3, a variable rule becomes more categorical as learners style-shift toward the IL superordinate. If in the initial stages of learning, the IL vernacular norm included a categorical rule specifying 0 percent of /r/, we might speculate that style shifting toward the IL superordinate would have entailed making that categorical rule more variable, by beginning to supply a small percentage of /r/.

It is important to point out here a major difference between paradigms 1 and 2 with regard to the nature of the variability which both paradigms agree exists. Paradigm 1 believes IL to be most permeable to invasion from other rule systems in *performance*—that is, in actually using the IL—and least permeable in the generation of grammatical intuitions. Paradigm 2 takes the opposite stance. Taking the third axiom of Labov's observer's paradox as being applicable to IL, it views the IL vernacular as being primary in the sense of being most stable and consistent; the vernacular style should evidence fewer target language or native language variants than the superordinate style (as accessible to intuitions, for example), and thus have greater internal consistency than the superordinate style.

In fact, the pattern we have observed in the data in Tables 1 to 6 is that the most careful style *is* most permeable to TL and NL (cf. pp. 4–14). As the learner pays increasing attention to language form, we may observe increasing evidence of TL and NL variants in his utterances.[11] The style in which the learner pays least attention to language form is the style with least evidence of invasion by other language systems, and the most evidence of structures which, like examples 10 and 11, seem related to neither NL nor TL, structures which arise spontaneously and which share features in common with pidgins, early child languages, and other "simplified" languages (Ferguson 1977). I have argued elsewhere (1982) that these research results so far support my own, and Dickerson's, claim that it is the vernacular IL style which is the most consistent and least permeable to outside influence (from TL/NL). This claim is empirically testable by means of future studies which gather more IL syntactic, morphological, and phonological data from a variety of elicitation tasks, including intuitional tasks and "free conversation" "tasks," and keep the data from these tasks separate in order to analyze the relative influence of TL, NL, and "pidgin-like" structures in each body of data.

Paradigm 2 views the IL vernacular style as that style which is least "permeable" in the sense of being more internally consistent, and evidencing fewer variants from the NL or the TL or other languages known to the learner. For paradigm 2 the vernacular styles is the baseline of variability. Paradigm 1, in contrast, views the IL careful style (as revealed in the grammatical intuitions of the learner) as being the least "permeable," and takes this as the baseline. The data we have examined in this paper support paradigm 2 rather than paradigm 1.

Paradigm 2 defines IL as the abstract capability which guides the regular language behavior of the second language learner. This capability is hypothesized to be an idealized linguistic system consisting of a continuum of styles; the system exists apart from any particular instance of its use. That portion of this continuum which underlies a particular instance of regular learner behavior may be determined by the degree of attention which the learner pays to language form in that instance.

Paradigm 2 is more constrained than paradigm 1 in that it makes predictions which are not made by paradigm 1. Specifically, paradigm 2 predicts that the IL casual style will evidence more pidgin-like forms traceable to neither NL not TL, while the careful style will be more permeable to influence from outside systems like NL and TL. Paradigm 1 does not make this prediction. Further, paradigm 2 predicts that shifting from casual to careful styles will be rule-governed, while paradigm 1 does not.

Paradigm 3: Dual Knowledge

Paradigm 3 has been proposed by Krashen (1981 and elsewhere), Bialystok (1981), and others. The version to be explored here will be Krashen's monitor theory. Paradigms 2 and 3 share several important assumptions and are much closer to each other than either is to paradigm 1. However, there are several important assumptions which differ between these two paradigms, and these differing assumptions result in differing abilities to deal with the data.

Assumption 1: Two Knowledge Systems. In paradigm 3, there are two completely independent systems of knowledge which make up the IL of the second language learner: an implicit knowledge system which consists of the unconscious knowledge of how to produce utterances, and a metalinguistic knowledge system which consists of knowledge about the language being learned. Krashen terms the second body of knowledge the Monitor; the Monitor is accessible to conscious introspection and may be described by the learner in terms of consciously formulated grammatical rules. These two knowledge systems seem to be homogeneous in Krashen's formulation; that is, each body of knowledge seems to be made up of a single set of invariant rules.

Note the fundamental differences between paradigms 3 and 2 with regard to the nature of the system being modeled by the researcher. Paradigm 3 views the system as essentially two independent systems, each of which is apparently homogeneous, and only one of which actually generates utterances. Paradigm 2 views the system as a single continuum of styles, all of which are related to one another and all of which may underlie utterances. We shall see that these different views of the nature of the system being modeled will lead to different treatments of variability, and that paradigm 3 cannot handle the variable data we are concerned with as well as paradigm 2.

Assumption 2: What Guides IL Behavior. In paradigm 3, the learner's implicit knowledge system actually initiates IL utterances in performance. The learner can modify the output of the implicit "grammar" by invoking rules from the metalinguistic knowledge system (the monitor) under certain conditions: (1) when the learner has enough time to do so, (2) when the learner is focused on form, and (3) when the learner consciously knows the grammar rule in question.

Thus, in this paradigm it is at times the implicit knowledge system alone which underlies IL behavior, and at times it is the implicit knowledge system modified by the metalinguistic knowledge system which does so. Metalinguistic knowledge is available to the learner only as a monitor, and cannot initiate uttterances. The monitor can only modify, or filter, the utterances generated by the implicit knowledge system. While Krashen does allow for some self-correction in language behavior by means of the implicit knowledge system (as this also occurs in one's native language), there is little said about this phenomenon. The primary focus of paradigm 3 is on the distinction between the implicit knowledge system and the metalinguistic knowledge system.

Note the difference between paradigms here. Paradigm 1 assumes that competence is accessible to a different sort of introspection—the ability to have grammatical intuitions, not the ability to consciously know the grammatical rules.[12] Paradigm 1's competence is the knowledge which "generates" learner utterances; paradigm 3 postulates a truly metalinguistic knowledge system which does not initiate utterances. For paradigm 3, it is only the implicit knowledge system, not accessible to introspection, which initiates utterances. Both paradigms 3 and 1 share the notion of two (or more) grammatical systems underlying interlanguage behavior under certain circumstances; however, they differ in their characterization of the competing underlying grammatical systems and in their assumptions about the circumstances in which behavior is produced by two, rather than one, grammatical systems.

Paradigm 3's monitor is more or less equivalent to the extreme super-ordinate end of the continuum in paradigm 2; the two paradigms differ in that paradigm 2 assumes a single, systematic continuum underlying all learner language production, a continuum which is describable by rule, while 3 postulates two distinct systems underlying language production.

Assumption 3: IL Data. Paradigm 3 gathers data on the nature of each of the two knowledge systems. Data on the implicit knowledge system consist of those utterances produced (orally or in writing) by the learner when the learner (1) has not had much time, (2) was not focused on form, or (3) did not consciously know the grammatical rules involved. Data on the metalinguistic knowledge system consist of utterances produced when the learner is asked to think about correct grammatical form, is given lots of time to self-correct, and can be shown to consciously know the grammatical rules involved. Krashen (1981) and others have done many studies eliciting these two broad categories of data. There does not seem to be any attempt to gather data relevant to variability within the implicit knowledge system itself; rather this implicit knowledge system seems to be accessible to any data gathered in any situation, in any mode (oral/written)—as long as criteria 1 to 3 are met. Of course, these methods of data collection follow logically from what these researchers are interested in showing—that there is a dichotomy between language produced under conditions considered appropriate for monitor use and that produced under other conditions. Variability under these other conditions is apparently not relevant within this paradigm.

Assumption 4: Nature and Cause of IL Variability. In paradigm 3, the only variability which is accounted for is the major dichotomy in the learner's language behavior when monitoring and when not monitoring. This dichotomy is considered to be due to the use or nonuse of the metalinguistic knowledge system. That is, monitoring, or the conscious application of grammatical rules, is conceived of as an either-or option, not as a continuum. While monitor theory also allows for "small-m" monitoring (which refers to paying attention to speech form), this notion is not developed to any great extent, nor does it have any impact on the way in which implicit knowledge is conceived of (i.e., implicit knowledge seems to be conceived of as homogeneous) or result in any care taken to distinguish among various kinds of data gathered in unmonitored learner language. Herein lies the major difference between paradigms 2 and 3. Paradigm 2 is concered with accounting for variability in IL along the full range of speech performance and conceives of the underlying IL capability as an unbroken continuum of speech styles. It views the generation of intuitions of grammaticality as another type of learner performance which provides access to the extreme superordinate end of the IL continuum. Paradigm 3, however, is primarily concerned with the difference between learner performance under very constrained circumstances (generous time allowance, attention paid to form, conscious knowledge of rule) and learner performance under *all other circumstances*. It is concerned with this difference because of its postulation of two underlying and independent grammatical systems, each of which is apparently homogeneous in nature.

The data in Tables 1, 3, and 4 are very important here, because they show more than just two dichotomous speech styles used by learners, and to that degree they provide support for paradigm 2 over paradigm 3. More data of the sort in Table 1 are clearly needed to provide support for one or the other paradigm. Evidence for paradigm 2 would be found if we could show that a structure initially incorporated into the extreme superordinate end of the continuum (and produced under conditions for monitor use) *gradually* moved from right to left along the continuum in Table 7. Evidence for paradigm 3 would be found if such a structure occurred first in the monitor and then did not gradually move along a continuum but rather suddenly appeared in the vernacular; this would provide evidence that two separate and distinct knowledge systems were involved.

Table 7.   Interlanguage Continuum

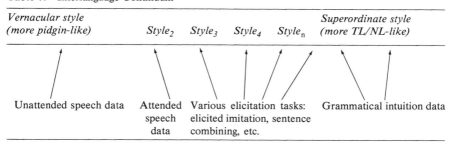

| *Vernacular style* *(more pidgin-like)* | *Style₂* | *Style₃* | *Style₄* | *Styleₙ* | *Superordinate style* *(more TL/NL-like)* |

| Unattended speech data | Attended speech data | Various elicitation tasks: elicited imitation, sentence combining, etc. | | | Grammatical intuition data |

CONCLUSION

Interlanguage data from several studies have been presented, and these data show that IL speech production varies systematically with elicitation task. This variability of IL is problematic for a theory of interlanguage because

1. Use of one or another task may lead to contradictory claims about the structure of interlanguage, so that we must decide what are the *best* data to use to characterize IL.
2. The kind of linguistic system hypothesized by the theory as underlying these learner utterances must be able to account for this variability. A model of this system must accurately describe and predict the systematic variability which takes place.

A review of three paradigms for the study of interlanguage has shown that the different assumptions these paradigms make about the nature of the underlying IL system lead to different decisions about the best data to use to characterize IL. The data gathered by each paradigm tend to reinforce that paradigm's basic assumption about the nature of the underlying IL system being modeled.

It has been argued that the data presented in Tables 1 to 6 can be described and predicted best by a model of IL which follows the assumptions of paradigm 2. The other paradigms cannot account for these data as accurately or as elegantly.

More data of the sort in Tables 1 to 6 are needed in order to validate the claims of one or another of these paradigms relative to one another. In particular, longitudinal studies which use a variety of elicitation tasks, and keep the data from these tasks separate from one another, may most effectively be used to determine which of these three paradigms is most adequate for the study of interlanguage.

Appendix.   (Simplistic) Outline of Three Paradigms for Interlanguage Study

Paradigm 1: homogeneous competence	Paradigm 2: capability continuum	Paradigm 3: dual knowledge
What is being modeled		
Homogeneous system of knowledge: competence	System consisting of range of styles, which guides regular language behavior of learner: capability	Dual system: 1. Metalinguistic knowledge 2. Implicit knowledge
What guides IL language behavior		
IL competence (above) *plus* invading systems in performance	IL capability (above)	Implicit knowledge optionally monitored by metalinguistic knowledge

Best data for study of IL

Combined data: primarily intuitional judgments; but data from tasks, utterances, etc., added in	Data kept *separate:* unattended utterances, attended utterances, elicitation tasks, intuitional judgments	Two kinds of data kept *separate:* 1. Unattended utterances 2. Monitored productions

How IL is internalized

?	Two ways: 1. Initial appearance of structure in unattended style 2. Gradual movement of structure from attended to unattended style	Two ways: 1. Implicit knowledge is unconsciously "acquired" 2. Metalinguistic knowledge is consciously "learned"

Cause of IL variability

Permeability: invasion of IL system by other rule systems in performance. Least permeability in intuitions (and careful speech?)	Variable style shifting due to attention shifts. Most permeability in intuitions and careful speech	Dichotomous performance due to use or nonuse of monitor under specific conditions

IL universals

IL obeys language universals, as a natural language	IL obeys language universals, as a natural language. Most structures like those in pidgins, early child language, etc., occur in unattended style	?

Uniqueness of ILs

IL is unique, qualitatively different in: 1. Permeability 2. Backsliding 3. Fossilization	IL is only quantitatively different from any other natural language	?

NOTES

1. My thanks to faculty and students of the Linguistics Department at the University of Minnesota—especially Jerry Sanders, Michael Kac, and Jan Smith—for helpful comments on an earlier draft of this paper. Thanks also to Grant Abbott, Richard Allwright, and Stig Eliasson. Errors and inconsistencies are of course my own.

2. While the notion of interlanguage is considered in theory to concern itself with both the speech production and the speech perception of second language learners, in fact, most research is done on speech production. This is probably because it is easier to study speech production in an interlingual domain, and much harder to find ways of studying what learners are perceiving apart from their abilities to produce speech in interlanguage. The paradigms discussed in this paper should be taken to refer to speech production only; their relevance to speech perception remains to be investigated.

3. Subsequent discussions by Selinker and collegues may be found in Tarone, Frauenfelder, and Selinker (1976), where we find statements like these: "There exists a separate linguistic or psycholinguistic system (interlanguage) which forms in the mind of the learner and which may take

the form of a pidgin and which may develop into a separate dialect in its own right. This system draws on both the NL and TL, as well as other sources for its surface forms." In this paper we call learner speech "systematic" when it evidences an internal consistency in the use of forms at a single point in time.

4. Nemser (1971) and others have argued that interlanguage is to be described not as a language of the individual but rather as a language with its own speech community. I find it difficult to distinguish this notion of IL from the notion of pidgin. Further, if one looks at a classroom filled with students who speak several native languages and make different errors in attempting to speak a target language, it is hard to imagine how this group might be called a "speech community," though I would still want to say that each individual is using an interlanguage in attempting to communicate in the TL.

5. It should be pointed out here that this third assumption does not logically follow from the first and second. In theory, one could use another source of data to model the native speaker's competence. But in fact all three assumptions have usually been accepted as a unit by those who use the Chomskian paradigm. (I am grateful to Gerald Sanders for making this point.) The usual rationale for preferring intuitional data is that other kinds of data are subject to random "performance" flaws like slips of the tongue, or to sociolinguistic variation not of interest to the linguist. Intuitions, on the other hand, have been viewed as basically independent of the influence of social situation. Recent work by Carroll et al. (1981) has called this last view into question.

6. My thanks to Kate Winkler for providing English translations of Adjémian's (1982) paper.

7. The same objections can of course be raised to the use of this paradigm for the study of first language acquisition as well. Because this paper focuses on problems for the study of *second* language acquisition, the objections are stated here solely in terms of the SLA situation.

8. How continuous is the continuum? How many styles should it contain to be truly considered a "continuum"? This, it seems to me, is an empirical question. The point is that if we work within a paradigm which postulates the existence of a continuum, we will design our studies in such a way as to test that postulation; instead of pooling results from various elicitation devices, we will try to keep these results separate and examine them to determine whether indeed they relate to one another as predicted. Allwright points out that it may turn out that intuitions of grammaticality will actually fall off the end of this continuum—that is, there may be a real dichotomy between what learners judge grammatical in some cases and what they can actually perform, even in their most careful style. This would occur if a learner could judge a TL sentence grammatical but be utterly unable to produce that sentence even with maximum attention paid to speech form. Or, more likely, it would occur if one could perceive a sound as being a correct TL sound but be unable to produce it. This problem returns us to the question of how perception in IL relates to production in IL (see footnote 2).

9. Other kinds of variability do occur. For example, learners may master more than one register of the TL, and use these appropriately in formal or informal situations. The *sort* of style shifting I discuss here is different from this kind of register shifting, though it may be related to it. The sort of style shifting I discuss here may take place *within* a single register of the TL; indeed, since most second language learners in the classroom are exposed to only one register of the TL, it is very likely that they know only one register. They may pay greater or less attention to language form as they use that register. As more registers of TL are mastered, the sort of style shifting I discuss here may interact with register shifting, just as it must in the native language.

10. Here, the reader may want to refer back to the distinction between *rules* and *regularities* (p. 15 and footnote 9) in considering a question raised by Sanders (personal communication): "What is the speaker really doing here? . . . applying a rule 50% of the time because he knows that 50% r occurrence is right for free speech?" The "rules" referred to here in paradigm 2 are perhaps better viewed as "regularities" in the sense that they describe patterns in observed behavior which are regular, and do not make claims about "what the learner is doing" because he "knows" a form is "right."

11. The case of phonology may be somewhat different from the case of morphology and syntax, in that one would expect on the basis of anecdotal evidence that the casual style for phonology should be most closely identified with TL—except for cases of prestige NL variants, as

we have seen. However, data like those of Johansson (1973) show that certain trends seemed to be present in IL phonology independently of NL and some long and back vowels seemed to be difficult for all learners, regardless of NL; there was a general tendency among all learners, regardless of NL, to "move from the extreme higher and lower positions in the articulation area toward the middle height, the tongue's rest position" (p. 151). One would want to know whether this tendency is more pronounced in casual styles than in careful styles; paradigm 2 would predict that it would be.

2 Memory, Learning, and Acquisition

Earl W. Stevick
Department of State

Let me make clear the basis on which I propose to approach the topic of this paper. Although I will be discussing memory, I obviously cannot speak as a psychologist, which I am not and never have been. Nor, in discussing the learning and acquisition of language, will I be speaking as a linguist. I was once a linguist, but that designation has pretty well lapsed. It lapsed in the mid-1960s, when my job took me into the maelstrom of Peace Corps language training. Negatively, I simply did not have time to try to keep up with linguistic science during those days. On the positive side, I saw so many successful language programs, and so many failures, by so many methods, with no obvious relationship between method and results, that I concluded there must be something other than linguistic analyses or pedagogical formulas which was making the difference. It was for that reason, I think, that when my Peace Corps activities began to slack off in the early seventies I turned, not back to linguistic science but to looking at work that had been going on in some widely separated corners of the field of psychology. Having given up calling myself a linguist, and never hoping to call myself a psychologist, I became an explorer of terra incognita in the world of adult learning of foreign languages.

What I have to present, then, is by way of an updated report on what I think I am finding out on my daily hikes across terrain that contains my own experiences as a language learner, my own work as a consultant to numerous teaching programs and materials development teams, my work as a materials writer, as a teacher, and as supervisor and observer of more teachers in more languages than I can count, twenty years of watching students learn that the Swahili word for "house" is *nyumba*, and that *mazungumza* is the word for "conversation." It also contains interviews with numerous students and teachers. Relatively recently, my explorations have been illuminated by limited but careful reading of some work in experimental psychology. Nevertheless, the terrain itself is not either psychology or linguistics; it is real people learning real languages for real jobs overseas. I will present my findings not in a convenient two-dimensional form such as would fit easily between the covers of proper scientific dispute but largely in the form of metaphor, for that is the way my mind works. I am a practitioner and not very much of a researcher. Maybe it is just as well I left linguistics and didn't try to enter psychology.

MEMORY

The most basic facts about memory, attested by research as well as by daily experience, are perhaps only three in number. The first is so obvious that it may seem unworthy of discussion. I will discuss it anyway, because it is the most basic. It is simply that our minds are able to take in and store more than one thing at a time. For example, the reader is, at this moment, taking in visual stimuli from both the printed page and the environment, and he or she probably knows what time it is, and whether the room is hot or cold, and perhaps who is sitting or standing nearby. I will call all of these separate "items." All of the items which are stored at the same time constitute a single "configuration," which is the record of a single "experience."

The second fact about memory which I postulate as true for all learning styles is that when a particular item comes into the mind, from whatever source, it can call back—or, as we say, it can "remind us of"—earlier experiences which included that same kind of item. (I am not going to try to define the crucial expression "same kind of.") If, for example, someone were suddenly to produce before you a beanbag, you could cite other occasions on which you had handled or at least seen a beanbag.

The third basic fact about memory is that, once an earlier instance of an item has been recalled to mind, it tends to bring with it other items that were stored along with it in memory. This process is immediate and in fact virtually inevitable. For example, if a moment ago you did remember earlier experiences with beanbags, you almost certainly recalled something about the place and the approximate time, perhaps the other people involved, the color of the beanbag, and so on. In fact, this is essential to what we mean by "recalling an *other* experience." As students of memory have sometimes put it, items which are stored together tend to be recalled together.

Now I would like to suggest a word picture which reflects all three of these simple but fundamentally important facts. Let us imagine that as all of the dozens and hundreds of items come in at any given moment—visual, auditory, olfactory, tactile, visceral, and all the rest—let us imagine that all of these sensations are somehow stored on a single rigid, infinitesimally thin plastic transparency something like the ones that we use on overhead projectors, and that these transparencies are stacked on top of one another in long-term memory (LTM). If a stack of two or three such transparencies is held up to the light, it may be mistaken for a single transparency. When one such configuration—one such "transparency"—is in STM, then any one item in that configuration (that "transparency") has the power of bringing out of the files (i.e., out of LTM) one or more instances of the same kind of item, and along with it the whole configuration(s) of which that item was a part. This is true whether the first item has just come in as a part of a new sensory input, or whether it is part of a configuration (a "transparency") which itself has been pulled out of the LTM stack.

To leave the word picture for a moment and go back to the simple everyday example, a few paragraphs ago you remembered another beanbag, and perhaps that brought back the place where you played with it. But having recalled that place, you can probably come up with other things that happened there, other people who shared in the game, and so on.

It also seems to be the case that the surface of any one such "transparency" is spattered with oil spots, so that some of the incoming items in a given experience adhere well and are easily available for later inspection, while other items that come in at the same time, from the same source, are for all practical purposes not registered. This effect shows up nowhere more clearly than in the learning of proper names or foreign vocabulary. In fact, the learning of foreign vocabulary is a rich mine of experiences which support the idea that we store even a relatively brief and clearly defined memory, such as an individual word, in the form of a number of separate propositions. These show up in the partially correct attempts at reproduction of words that we have met but not mastered. We can perform an informal experiment on that right here and now. A few paragraphs ago I noted two Swahili words with their English equivalents. The reader might take just a moment now to jot down, for his or her own use only, anything that he or she can about either the Swahili words or the English ones.

As far as the Swahili words are concerned, any resemblances between the forms read and the ones written down must be due either to chance or to something that was somehow retained. Yet in a word like *nyumba*, which has five phonemes, six letters, and even more phonological features, the number of potential points of similarity greatly exceeds the number of sounds or letters or features. We occasionally become conscious of such aspects of words while we are in the process of trying to reconstruct an earlier input. A few that I have caught myself using at one time or another are implied in the answers to the following questions:

Is it more than one syllable?
Is it less than four syllables?
Are the vowels in the word all alike?
Are there nasal consonants?
Are the consonants formed at the same point of articulation?
Do the vowels appear in the same order in some other word that I already know?

Let me emphasize here that this word picture is just that—a word picture and nothing more. By it, I do not mean to imply a view of memory as consisting of frozen sensory data. On the contrary, I intend this word picture to accommodate a constructivist view of memory. This is possible because the elements—the abstract elements—from which construction is to be carried out are included among the items which are registered on the "transparencies." Whatever partially incorrect versions of the Swahili words were produced, they were, after all, constructed consistent with whatever items were available from one reading of the word.

The process of going from present beanbag to remembered beanbag to remembered place to remembered people and so on may repeat itself spontaneously and very rapidly. The "transparency" metaphor therefore seems to me to be anything but static. Thus, one item may bring back another configuration ("transparency") in which it had occurred earlier, and a quite different item in that second transparency may bring back a third transparency in which *it* had occurred, and so on. When this process moves slowly enough so that we can be aware of it, we call it "free association," or we simply say that our mind is wandering. The same thing also goes on very, very rapidly all the time. Thus Woods (1980) is of the opinion that "conscious processing seems to be largely sequential and relatively slow, whereas the subconscious processes must (by virtue of the information-processing tasks that they accomplish) be either highly parallel or exceptionally fast (or both)."

I have implied that each item in a configuration tends to bring back one or many or all of the other configurations in which it had occurred earlier. I have also implied that once an item has been retrieved in this way, *it* brings with *it* many or even all or the other items that were stored on the same transparency with *it.* There is of course not room enough in consciousness—or in STM—for even a tiny fraction of the information that could come pouring back in this way. There is, however, considerable evidence that this sort of information can still influence behavior.

A simple example is found in an experiment by Meyer and Schvaneveldt, quoted in Bransford (1979). Subjects heard pairs of stimuli in which a word was followed either by another word or by a nonsense form. The subjects' task was to decide whether the second member of each pair was a word or not. The word *doctor*, for example, occurred as the second member of a pair following either *bread* or *nurse*. Subjects were accurate in idenitifying it as a word under both conditions, of course, but they were able to make the identification much more rapidly under the second condition. This sort of evidence—and there is much of it—suggests that each item in a recalled configuration affects the probability of recall of every other item in that same configuration. This is what has been called "priming," or "spreading activation" (Bransford 1979, 171ff.).

To change the metaphor, it is as though two items, once they have been together in consciousness at the same time, may ever thereafter remain connected by a slender thread. Just one of these threads by itself may not be strong enough to bring a second item back into consciousness, but it can draw it nearer, making it more readily available.

It is apparently items, and not whole stimuli, which are connected to one another. In the *house-nyumba* example, a person who came up with **nanda* would presumably have retained such items as "two syllables," "nasals in both syllables," "coarticulated nasal-voiced stop in second syllable," and "last vowel is -*a.*" The same person would have failed to retain such items as "the two vowels are different," "the two consonants are at different points of articulation," or "the noun contains the same root as the verb that means 'to form or shape.' " Again, let me emphasize that all these things that I am calling "items" are of kinds that I have actually found myself using spontaneously in learning new foreign language (FL) words.

One more essential point: the slender threads which connect contemporaneous items run out not only between, say, *house* and "nasals in both syllables," *house* and "same root as *to shape*," and so forth. They also run between "nasals in both syllables," and "same root as *to shape*," and all the rest. That is to say, these threads are not merely a set of radii all attatched to a single center, in this case the word "house." Instead, they make up a complex network, with a "thread" running from each such item to every other.

Some experimental work by Stein (1977) illustrates what I mean by a relatively powerful network, or web, of these interconnections. Subjects in one of two groups were presented with a list of 24 similes ("A pin is like a nail.") and were asked only to indicate whether they understood each of them. Later, the experimenter presented the subjects with the subject nouns from the simile sentences, and asked them to give the second noun in the pair. Performance was rather good.

To interpret this experiment in terms of the metaphor of networks or webs, let us suppose that a subject, on hearing the word "pin," generated a mental image which included among it at least dozens of items some visual and/or aural representation of the word itself, plus a picture of a pin, plus the items "sharp," "shiny," "metal," and "bendable." Similarly, the word "nail" would generate a visual and/or aural representation of the word, plus a picture of a nail, plus the items "sharp," "shiny," "metal," and "stiff." In the transparency metaphor, all these items—words, pictures, and all the rest—are stored on a single transparency. In terms of the web metaphor, there is a thread running from each of these items to each of the others.

Now what happens on the test, when the stimulus word "pin" is presented? For one thing, of course, the word will tend to bring back all or many of the items on the transparency that I have just described. But, needless to say, that word will also have other associations: "needle," "hem," "safety—," and many, many others. Items on the recent transparency, however, carry with them preexisting connections, based on previous experiences—what earlier we called "priming." The item "sharp," for example, will presumably bring with it such items as a tack, an awl, a razor, and of course, a nail. Each of these images, since the test is in the subjects' native language, in turn brings with it its name. Similarly "shiny" may bring a button, a badge, and a nail, and "metal" may bring wire, iron, and nail. Many of these items that were generated by the simile sentence point to "nail," and few or none to "hem" or "safety." The combined strength of all these "threads" was for many subjects sufficient to pull the word "nail" back under the conditions of the experiment.

Such a network is obviously much stronger and more stable than a simple set of radii would have been. It is nevertheless quite fragile. To leave the metaphor again and go back for a moment into the real world, we seldom have very good recall of a word that we have met casually and only once. But, back in the metaphor now, if each of the items can call back earlier instances of the same item, and if these earlier items were related in the same configuration as the present experiences are—if they are connected in a similar network—then the two networks, incomplete though they are, will begin to support each other, and to form a readily available framework to which missing items may attach themselves. Eventually, after enough experiences and perhaps a little conscious cognitive processing, we assemble networks which are able to produce accurate, dependable, and rapid retrieval. (I gave an example of this "assembling" process on p. 43 of Stevick 1982.)

I have said that the process of association moves spontaneously and rapidly, and so it does. This does not mean, however, that it is either an autonomous process or an aimless kaleidoscope. The effect of intentional cognitive processing is shown in the results obtained by the other group of subjects in Stein's experiment. This second group was not asked to try to understand the simile. They were asked only to say whether the two items in each sentence were relatively hard or relatively soft. This required them to visualize the items, of course, and to perform a certain amount of cognitive processing on them, but it apparently did not lead to the richer processing that the open-ended instruction had produced. The cued recall scores of this second group were less than half the scores of the first group.

Returning now to the "transparency" metaphor, let us look at a fourth fact about memory. This fourth fact has to do with the nature of the items that are stored in these configurations, or on these "transparencies." They of course include shapes and textures and times of day—things drawn directly from the interpretation of sensory data. As I have already suggested they also include abstractions from these data: the fact that the shrubs get smaller as we move away from the house, or that all the digits in this phone number are even, for example.

Further—and this is of utmost importance—they include purposes and expected outcomes, as well as the abstractions that will be necessary for the construction of schemata and scripts. I have also said that they include emotions and visceral reactions. This great heterogeneity of items may exist on various levels and for all I know may be stored in quite different ways. What I am saying is that all of them are stored in the same configurations and participate in the same "networks" and (or "and therefore") can serve as reminders of one another. This feature of memory extends far beyond the language classroom, of course. Much poetry and all metaphor depend on it, too.

Now I would like to give a more extended classroom example. Imagine a language classroom in which a student has been studying Spanish vocabulary by the most primitive of paired-associate techniques. When the teacher says "house," the student replies "casa," and when the teacher says "casa," the student replies "house," and so on for other pairs of words. If in fact the student has been storing a series of configurations—transparencies—while this was going on, then a number of those transparencies will contain the item "house." When this same item appears on the quiz a few days later, it will tend to bring back those particular transparencies, and on them will of course also appear, in the section reserved for Spanish, the word "casa." If all goes smoothly, the student merely looks at the transparency (or, more likely, at the stack of transparencies) that contain "house," copies off the Spanish equivalent onto the exam paper, and everyone lives happily ever after.

When a student who has learned in this way goes out into the world and sees a real house and wants to talk about it in Spanish, he or she is first reminded of the English word, which then helps to bring back the needed Spanish word. The circuitousness of this linkage has of course long been the target of criticism on the part of practitioners of various forms of the direct method.

In a slightly more sophisticated technique, pictures of houses take the place of the Spanish word. Now, the ex-student who is walking down the street and who wants to talk about a nearby house has available for this purpose a number of transparencies which contain the object and also contain the foreign word without any mediation from the native language. This is undeniably an improvement over the first technique.

Much of the research on memory in the FL classroom has in fact been concerned with differences of technique which are comparable with the difference which I have just described, even though some of the variations of material and procedure have been much more ingenious and effective than the two that I have stated here. What they have in common is that they focus on just two parts of each transparency: the word or the structural pattern to be learned, and the item or items which *directly correspond* to it either in the student's native language or in the outside world.

But if what I said above is true, then this limited focus is not consistent with the nature of the transparencies—with the nature of the stored memory configurations. Two points in particular stand out. First, the configurations— the transparencies—inevitably contain countless other items besides those two on which language teachers are accustomed to focusing. Second, all the items in a given transparency, or in fact in a given stack of related transparencies, tend to call to mind all of the other items that have occurred along with them.

LEARNING AND ACQUISITION

With these two points in mind, let us go back and look at the first primitive technique that I described above. The English word "house" will serve as a reminder for "casa," all right, but it was also associated with, and will be a reminder for, the classroom walls, and the 10:00–11:00 class hour, and the teacher's face, and the purpose of being credited with a right answer, and all the rest. The classroom wall, once recalled to memory in this way, will in turn serve as a reminder for "casa" *and* for the 10:00 hour *and* for the teacher's face, and so on. What we have here, as I put it in my second metaphor, is a whole network of mutual remindings—all very cozy.

One thing that makes this cozy arrangement less than ideal, of course, is the fact that there is more than one word or one grammatical structure in the target language. The English words "city" and "table" and "pencil" will bring back the same ambient items of location and time and purpose, and these ambient items, whether they were recalled by "city" or by "table" or by "pencil" or by "house," will tend equally to bring back "lapiz" *and* "casa" *and* "mesa" *and* "ciudad." In this sense I would like to say that such a configuration, or such a stack of transparencies, is poorly "integrated" within itself.

Now let us take a look at what happens when a child is mastering its first language. The physical locations, the types of activity, the purposes, and many other parts of the configuration(s) that are stored along with instances of the word "house" will on the average be quite different from the physical locations and the types of activity and the purposes and all the rest that are stored along with instances of "pencil," for example. Moreover, the other (the nonlinguistic) items on the transparencies that contain "casa" will generally be good reminders for one another. What is essential to my argument is that the items on the transparency that contains "casa" will be *better* reminders for one another than they will be for "lapiz" *or* for the nonlinguistic items that are frequent on the transparencies that contain "lapiz." The reverse applies from "lapiz" to "casa." The networks of mutual "reminding" are quite different in the stacks of transparencies that contain the two words. Contrast this with the primitive technique that I described earlier, in which the two networks were over-whelmingly alike. In this sense, the configurations that the child takes in as it meets its native language may be said to be "well integrated."

A well-integrated configuration, then, is one in which the items are good reminders of each other, and not of a number of other false targets. To put the same thing in another way, a configuration may be "integrated" with respect to a particular item, called the "target," which it contains. The degree to which one item is a reminder for another depends (partly) on the number of times that the target item appears on transparencies which are members of the small stack of transparencies which are brought back by the reminding item. A transparency is "well integrated" with respect to a given target item if, first, it contains that item, and if moreover the other items in the transparency are good reminders of one another and of the target, and not of a number of spurious targets.

There are three features which make a well-integrated configuration superior to a poorly integrated configuration when it comes to the practical use of a language. First, there is a better signal-to-noise ratio; that is, there is a higher proportion of other items pointing to the desired item, relative to the proportion of other items which point equally to undesired items. In the example that I used, the walls of the classroom tend to bring back "lapiz" and "ciudad" and "mesa" just as much as they tend to bring back "casa." Second, the ambient items—particularly the purposes—on a well-integrated transparency are those which occur in real life: finding shelter, for example, or finding something to write with, rather than the purpose of coming up with the correct equivalent of some English word or other. This means that these same nonlinguistic surroundings and these same purposes, when they recur in the future, will have the property of making more accessible the linguistic items that should go with them.

As for the third advantage of well-integrated configurations, notice also what happens when a language has been learned in terms of transparencies of the poorly integrated variety. Any word in the FL will have been stored with, and so will tend to reawaken, whatever feelings of anxiety or boredom or caution may have been present in the academic setting, including the motivation of avoiding errors. Well-integrated configurations ought therefore to lead to greater fluency than poorly integrated ones do.

It must have been obvious to the reader for some time now that the type of poorly integrated configuration that I have been discussing is the characteristic product of "learning," in the narrow sense of that term, and that well-integrated configurations are the normal outcome of "acquisition." If what I have said up to this point is true, then both "learning" and "acquisition" are examples of a single process operating under different circumstances.

This fundamental unity of "learning" and "acquisition" is the principal thesis that I wish to place before you, and I would like to explore a few possible corollaries of this position. First, though, I must hasten to point out that if I *am* right, and if "learning" and "acquisition" *are* at bottom the same thing, this still does not detract from the enormous practical importance of the distinction or even, on one level, from the theoretical usefulness of the two concepts.

I am proposing, then, to replace the two discrete processes called "learning" and "acquisition" with a contrast between "poorly integrated" and "well-integrated" configurations—actually families of related configurations which I have been picturing as "stacks" of "transparencies." What makes the difference, I am arguing, is the *degree* of integration. But "degree of integration" implies a continuum, and the idea of a continuum appeals strongly to my instincts as a language teacher. In this respect one learner may operate very close to the "acquisition" end of the continuum, a second may operate near the "learning" end, and a third may alternate rapidly between the two.

This range of styles was illustrated a few years ago in a series of interviews that I had with people who had been extraordinarily successful with foreign languages as adults. Three were particularly interesting because each of them began his or her account by observing that what he or she did was nothing special—just the "natural" way of going at a new language. One suceeded by merely associating with people informally and picking the language up in that way—a striking example of adult acquisition. Incidentally, this student was almost destroyed by being forced to participate in a class that did almost nothing but learning. The second of these three people considered the natural way to consist of sitting hour after hour across the table from a teacher, repeating words and sentences and being corrected. This of course is an extreme example of learning with little or no acquisition. The third person liked to become familiar with some new bit of structure or vocabulary either through elicitation or from a book, and then to make it permanent by going out and using it in genuine communicative interchange with nonteachers, thus using both types of technique.

The first teaching technique that I described was, as I stated, an extremely primitive one, chosen in order to illustrate one end of the learning-acquisition continuum. The experience of a person making his or her way out of infancy illustrates the other end of the same continuum. But few if any teachers have ever confined themselves to the first end, and few people except infants have available to them either the external support or the time required at the second end. Language teachers and language students have always operated somewhere in between. A recent formulation of this folk wisdom is Paulston and Bruder's (1976) tripartite distinction among "mechanical practice," "meaningful practice," and "communicative practice."

One activity which lies close to, but not at, the "learning" end of the continuum is a version of the well-known game "Concentration," as described in the Lifelines course by Foley and Pomann (1981). In this game, a number of pictures are affixed to cards, and the corresponding words are written on another set of cards. All cards are then turned face-down, the picture cards in one section and the word cards in another section. A student then turns over a word card and a picture card. If they match, the player keeps them, but if they do not match, the player turns them face down again and the next player takes a turn.

In this game, the student who turns over the word "table" must form in his or her mind a picture of this object so as to be able to compare that picture with the one on the card that he or she will turn up a moment later. As for purpose, it is no longer merely to get the next answer right. Instead, it is to complete and perhaps to win the game. Completing the game requires students to concentrate their attention on a particular set of facts (i.e., the arbitrary locations of the cards) which have no connection to the lexical equivalences which are its academic goal. The words thus become, as they are in real life, subordinate to some nonlinguistic purpose, even though this particular nonlinguistic purpose is not one that is found in everyday life.

Now, by way of contrast, here is a technique which lies close to but not at the "acquisition" end of the continuum. The class is given a brief story with no ending. Two alternative endings are proposed either in written form or orally by the teacher. Students work in small groups and then as a full class to discuss which of the two endings is the more plausible. In this technique, the students must first form in their minds pictures which correspond to/are consistent with the story fragment, and other sets of pictures which are consistent with the two endings. They must next compare the three to a plethora of transparencies which represent their total experience of the world so far, and decide which combination fits best. Finally, they must listen to one another's words, convert other people's words into pictures, and compare those pictures with their own.

Among the purposes that will become items on the new transparencies that are formed during this process are gathering information, making judgements, and persuading. These are purposes which occur every day in life outside the classroom. This technique nevertheless falls short of pure acquisition insofar as the gathering, judging, and persuading are motivated not by the basic physical, economic, or emotional needs of life, but by academically created facsimiles of those needs.

Now consider the plight of a new item—say, a new foreign word—which occurs for the first time in a setting where acquisition rather than learning is going on. The item is stored on a transparency which is in general very well integrated. Yet, since this is the first appearance of the item in question, it does not bring with it a stack of older transparencies. This means that it does not bring with it any indicators of how it fits into the world in general or into this transparency in particular. The word may therefore prove to be very hard—for practical purposes impossible—to retrieve when it is next needed. If it does not recur fairly soon, it might almost as well never have been met at all. This is of course one way of accounting for the fact that second language acquisition is a slow process relative to the rapid short-term results that can often be achieved through learning.

What I have just said about the acquisition of new words is even more true of the acquisition of new patterns and new schemata. Patterns by definition cannot be experienced in a single instance. A pattern is after all a relationship of similarity between two relationships of difference. An extremely simple example is found in that fact that the English consonants p and b are different from each other, and the consonants t and d are different from each other, but the way in which they differ is the same.

On the other hand, as those of us who have tried to teach foreign languages to other people know all too well, a pattern that is clearly introduced today, and thoroughly drilled tomorrow, may for all practical purposes be gone the day after tomorrow—or even after class tomorrow—because it had not been made a part of well-integrated configurations, including motives, which are essential parts of real, nonacademic language use.

What learning *can* produce, to use the metaphor of transparencies, is a transparency or a small stack of transparencies in which the *form* of the new item (word, pattern, or schema) is clear, and it can generally do this much more readily than acquisition can. What it does *not* do, as I have already said, is integrate this form with the full range (or even a partial range of any considerable size) of circumstances and purposes for which it would be appropriate in the spontaneous usage of language in life outside the classroom.

Given this combination of strengths and weaknesses for learning and for acquisition, it is sometimes expedient to use both processes in a way which will allow them to complement each other. In particular, one can produce by language a small stack of transparencies—that is, a series of poorly integrated but very clearly delineated experiences that are close to one another in time—

which then, before they are lost in the nether reaches of the LTM stack, can be grafted or spliced into other transparencies—other experiences—of the acquisition type.

The two processes of learning and acquisition may also be combined in the opposite order. Words and patterns which have come up in an acquisition-type experience may be picked out and made the center of less well-integrated experiences which serve to clarify them. The new, clearer, more complete record of the new item then becomes available for recall when next the item is needed either for comprehension or for production in a communicative setting.

CONCLUSION

In what I have discussed, I have really introduced no new facts. It is after all well known that one instance of an item can bring back other instances of the same item, and that recall of one item can do the same for other, dissimilar items that occurred with it at some time in the past. It is also well known that items which are recalled in this way can influence perception and behavior without themselves crossing the threshold into consciousness. These are, after all, elementary principles of an old and simple brand of psychology. All that I have tried to do is, first, to push these simple principles perhaps a bit farther than we ordinarily do; second, to emphasize how numerous are the kinds of data that we store; and third, to make clear what I mean by the degree to which a set of inputs which occur together in the mind are "integrated" with one another. I have concluded by suggesting that what we have been calling the "learning" and the "acquisition" of languages may be seen as a single process working itself out under different sets of circumstances—circumstances which are not "either-or" but which vary along a continuum. In this interpretation, there is no need to decide whether learning can contribute to acquisition, or whether acquisition can contribute to learning. The role of the pedagogue becomes that of finding out (or of guessing) which transparencies are available to a given group of students at a given time, and of seeing how these transparencies may be connected with one another, and then of guiding the progressive relating of these transparencies and new transparencies (experiences) so as to approach some set of agreed-on goals.

3 Processing Universals in Second Language Acquisition

Herbert W. Seliger
Queens College
City University of New York

In attempting to explain rather than describe second language acquisition, the researcher is faced with three paradoxes:

1. The first paradox might be referred to as the problem of looking at everything but seeing little. What does one look at and what relative value does one place on findings? Second language acquisition (SLA) research has been blessed with copious and rich output, but it is not clear what should be done with it. What is the explanatory power of our findings? Is everthing equally relevant for explaining SLA? How do we decide what is important and what is not?

2. The second paradox might be called the paradox of acquisition itself. Can the mind be occupied with acquisition and the normal processing of input and output at the same time? Research cited by Sharwood-Smith (1981) indicates that memory for surface structure is short-lived. That is, surface structure is discarded as soon as it is recorded at the semantic level. If this is true, how is it possible to acquire syntax, since the *form* of the sentence is quickly discarded? One must conclude that an adequate model of SLA must distinguish between those processes carried out in normal language communication and the process of acquisition itself. That is, an adequate model must distinguish between what are commonly called "communication strategies" and those responsible for acquisition (see Selinker and Lamendella 1979 and Tarone 1980 for a discussion of this).

3. The third paradox that any model of SLA must deal with is that concerned with the conflict between the perspective of the observer/researcher and the perspective of the learner. Faerch and Kasper (1980) have noted this. How can the observer know what is going on in the mind of the learner? For that matter, how can learners know what is going on in their own mind at other than a superficial level of consciousness? SLA research has been witness to some rather questionable pronouncements in this area of late. (See Cohen and Hosenfeld 1981 on the uses of "mentalistic" data in SLA research.)

A central problem which faces anyone who attempts to explain SLA is that it is so variable while at the same time being the same. That is, there are a wide variety of contexts and circumstances within which SLA can happen as well as variability in terms of the learners themselves. Much of the research in the field has been devoted to examining or identifying these variables. Our literature is rich with studies of good learners and bad learners, risk takers, child and adult comparisons, comparisons of learners from different L1s, and so on. The truth may be that the more we find out about L2 acquisition and the more our research continues in this direction, the more hopeless our situation seems to become. That is, the more variables we identify the more we attempt to explain the combinations of these variables through the wonders of the computer and multivariate analysis.

Given a plethora of theories and learner characteristics and behaviors, we are faced with the impossible task of knowing how to evaluate findings and how to place them in their right perspective. While many characteristics have been identified with language learners and in some cases these characteristics have been related correlationally to language achievements, we have no mechanism for deciding which of the phenomena described or reputed to be carried out by the learner are in fact those that lead to language acquisition. Surely, if it is found that good language learners breathe deeply before producing a hypothesis, the implication is that this must be related to SLA. From here it is but a short step to identifying all kinds of things that learners do while in a language learning context from head scratching, eyebrow raising, and pupil dilation to reporting what one had for lunch or thinking about experiences of the night before.

The point is that learners do an infinite variety of things while in the process of learning a language. The likelihood, however, is that some of their activity may be meaningful to the process of acquisition while other aspects of it may be, in the communication theory sense, simply noise. It should be a truism that because so many things are happening at once, not only observers but also learners themselves cannot possibly be aware of what is going on. Only some learner activity may be regarded as contributing to effecting change in the memory processes that represent the evolving interlanguage grammar.

The model in Figure 1 is an attempt to relate the many and diverse aspects of SLA while providing a framework which recognizes that in spite of such infinite diversity there exists the universal fact that human beings of all ages, attitudes, levels of intelligence, socioeconomic background, etc., succeed in acquiring L2s in a wide variety of both naturalistic and formal settings.

The model attempts to explain why not everything that L2 learners do leads to acquisition, why some activities lead to long-term increments in the interlanguage grammar while others simply lead to short-term language-like performance.

In attempting to deal with the other paradoxes mentioned above, the model recognizes that some levels of acquisition processing cannot be examined or observed in any direct sense, any more than competence can, and must be inferred on the basis of external evidence while those aspects of acquisition processing which are observable or reportable through introspection by learners are limited in their validity and may in fact lead to invalid conclusions about acquisition.

The model predicates the existence of basically two levels of acquisition processing: one level, called *strategy*, is universal, age- and context-independent, and when engaged must be assumed to lead to long-term acquisition. The second level, called *tactic*, consists of what might be considered an infinitely variable set of behaviors or learning activities dependent on a wide variety of factors such as environment, age, personality, affective constraints, and first language. In fact, it might be argued that the features which determine the second tier of activity, tactics, would constitute a catalogue of learner variables found in SLA literature.

These two levels of processing, strategy and tactic, may be predicated on two premises which may be stated about language and second langauge acquisition.

Premise 1. The specific circumstances under which language may be learned are almost unlimited in terms of the possible combinations of learner variables, target and source language variables, and social and educational variables. Language may be learned in school as a foreign language, in the jungle by people with no formal education, by learners with all levels of intelligence, and even by learners without live interlocutors.

What Premise 1 states is that it is impossible to describe all the variables for language learning. It may be possible to state many of the variables for a specific instance of language learning but even here it is unlikely that all variables can be identified or accounted for. It follows from Premise 1 that the more variables we discover, the more difficult the task becomes in accounting for the combinations of these variables in different constellations.

A corollary assumption of Premise 1 must be that the mechanisms responsible for extracting the same basic underlying principles of language from all this variability must be both limited in scope in order to be useful for such a wide variety of learners and universal so that a shared system of communication operating in the same manner will evolve at the end of the process.

Premise 2. All human languages are structured so as to be learnable by the same universal acquisition mechanisms. All languages take into consideration real human limitations in processing such as limits on recursiveness, self-embeddings, and length of utterance. Languages appear to be structured so that they are amenable to chunking into semantically discrete units appropriate to the short-term memory capacity of the learner be he or she adult or child.

There is, in other words, a direct relationship between the codes which humans acquire and the mechanisms used to acquire these codes. Languages must have built into them the potential for their learnability or they would cease to exist. While we could conceivably memorize, through the use of brute memory, strings much longer than the magic number seven plus or minus two (Miller 1956), we could not memorize enough of these strings to match real language ability. The demands of communication would quickly exceed the

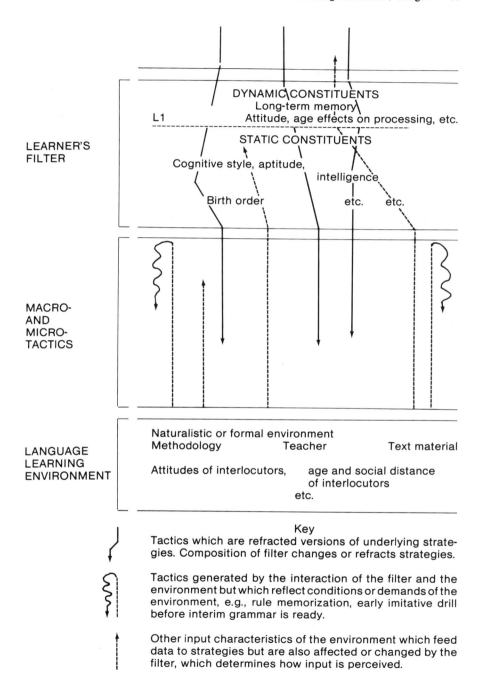

FIGURE 1.   Biologically Determined Learning Strategies

ability of memory to store all the units which have to be memorized and mated to appropriate discourse and sociolinguistic cues. For this reason the memorization of dialogues cannot be said to represent real language acquisition. Since we approach languages as codes which contain underlying abstract principles, what must be learned is the abstract key which can be stored within a given memory capacity.

A corollary of Premise 2 is that all normal human beings are capable of learning a *second* language. While this is a direct outcome of the assumption embedded in Premises 1 and 2, there are also important qualifications which must be kept in mind.

1. Factors which are determined by age or context such as sociologically induced attitudes, pedagogically induced modes of acquisition, or individually preferred pathways for dealing with a specific language acquisition context will not be the same for any two individual learners. In terms of the strategy/tactic dichotomy, this would mean that while at the level of tactic there will be very wide variability, language acquisition of some form will result when strategies are engaged.

2. The corollary to Premise 2, that all human beings are capable of learning a second language, does not imply any minimum or maximum level of acquisition. The same basic processes, strategies, are involved in learning a limited system as well as acquiring a more elaborate system. There is no absolute size to an interlanguage grammar. A limited small grammar contains all the necessary characteristics of a large extended grammar in terms of basic cognitive processes, strategies, required and must be acquired in the same way. In terms of the strategies used to acquire language, the same abstract set is used from beginning knowledge through advanced knowledge. In this sense, the difference between the good language learner and the poor language learner is in the tactics used rather than the strategies used.

STRATEGY

The strategy level of acquisition processing is the most difficult to demonstrate, since it is not concerned with overt forms of behavior as in the case of some tactics. We must assume the existence of the strategy level based on premises about language and language learning made above.

This level has been described in various ways in the literature which attempts to explain how language acquisition takes place. Fodor (1980), taking an extreme nativist position, distinguishes between what he calls "fixation of belief" and true concept formation. However, he states that any learning theory must acknowledge among the processes involved hypothesis testing and confirmation (p.145). Lenneberg (1967) had referred to this level of strategy as "a ubiquitous process (among vertebrates) of categorization and extraction of similarities."

Strategies are the basic abstract categories of processing by which information perceived in the outside world is organized or categorized into cognitive structures as part of a conceptual network. This process is carried out through the mind's contrasting the known with the unknown and attempting to comprehend the unknown by relating it to what is already stored in long-term memory (Collins and Quillian 1972). The basic process for this procedure is hypothesis testing. Terms such as overgeneralization, language transfer, and simplification are necessarily variant forms of the matching and comparing which lead to hypotheses being formed, tested, and confirmed or rejected.

Looking at Figure 2, it might be claimed that, while the strategy level of acquisition is unconscious and abstract, there may be different levels of abstraction from simple pattern recognition and matching such as that carried out by the right hemisphere to hypothesis testing and confirmation specifically related to language and linguistic universals.

Based on the view presented here, since strategies are unconscious, innate, and involuntary, they cannot be taught nor can they be acquired in any way. This level of acquisition processing may be regarded as present in the mind and in operation when triggered by relevant data much as Lenneberg describes the acquisition device resonating to environmental stimulation. In this sense, studies of "good" language learners (Rubin 1981) or introspective research (Cohen and Hosenfeld 1981) will not provide any insights into the level of strategy. Since strategy is stimulated involuntarily, it is an empirical question as to which data trigger the hypothesis formation process. A research hypothesis,

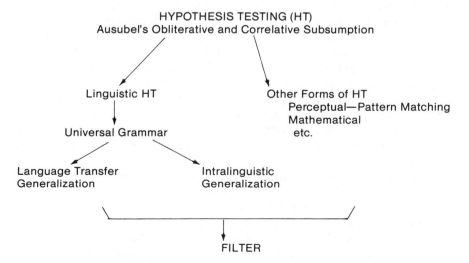

Assumptions: 1. Strategies are invariant and universal
              2. Data to which strategies apply dependent on contents of filter

HYPOTHESIS TESTING (HT)
Ausubel's Obliterative and Correlative Subsumption

Linguistic HT

Universal Grammar

Language Transfer
Generalization

Intralinguistic
Generalization

Other Forms of HT
Perceptual—Pattern Matching
Mathematical
etc.

FILTER

FIGURE 2.   Strategy Level of Processing (Possible Strategy Types)

then, would be that only certain kinds of language data could trigger the neuropsychological mechanism responsible for the cognitive act referred to metaphorically as strategy or specifically as hypothesis formation.

TACTIC

The second level of processing has been termed *tactic* to show its relationship to the long-term unchangeable form of internal processing, strategy, and to indicate that unlike strategy, tactic is affected by more immediate conditions which cannot always be predicted. Tactics evolve to meet the demands of the moment or fluctuate more slowly as a result of changes in attitude, maturation, general learning environment, or adjustments in the goals of the learner.

Tactics function at a macro level where a tactic may be responsible for setting up the situation so that the learner may then obtain data. An example of a macro-tactic would be the decision to learn the second language in a classroom or in a naturalistic environment. Tactics which function at the micro level provide direct input upon which learning strategies act. An example of a micro-tactic would be a learner's actual use of inferencing to determine the meaning of a specific language form.

THE LEARNER'S FILTER

The learner's filter (shown in Figure 1) provides for the interface between strategy level and the tactic level and is responsible for the idiosyncratic tactic style of individual learners. The filter explains why, when faced with the same learning task, different learners will approach the task differently even though the end result will be the same. The contents of the filter may consist of inherited or experientially acquired characteristics that affect the way one learns or approaches a particular learning task or problem. McCawley (1978) advocated "a conception of language acquisition in which many details of acquisition are random or are influenced by ephemeral details of one's linguistic experience." There is no reason to assume, given possible alternative analyses of language learner data, that all learners necessarily acquire a second language using the same methodology. Each learner's filter will determine just how underlying forms are finally arrived at.

The filter consists of static and semistatic or dynamic features which learners bring with them to each new learning situation and which determine how externally presented data will be perceived for the purposes of acquisition. The content of the filter will determine the learner's selection of preferred tactics. Since tactics obtain or provide data upon which the strategy level works, the filter may be said to be responsible for the individualized manner in which strategies are realized as tactics by learners.

Assumptions: 1. Idiosyncratic and variable
              2. Influenced by both filter and environment

MACRO-TACTICS

Activities which organize the learning situation, prepare the learner for actual processing, develop a set for acquisition processing.
Examples: 1. Noticing a foreign accent and listening for native speaker pronunciation
           2. Joining a L2 group of peers and "faking" L2 proficiency with prefabricated routines (Wong-Fillmore 1976)
           3. Asking to be corrected (Rubin 1981)
           4. Initiating conversations with L2 speakers

MICRO-TACTICS

Reflective

Controlled externally. Not motivated by internal need to learn but to satisfy transient external demands for performance.
Examples: 1. Memorization of dialogues
           2. Drill performance
           3. Lab pronunciation practice

Refractive

Motivated by internal need to "comprehend" environmentally triggered input. Concrete realization of hypothesis formation and testing.
Examples: 1. Hypothesizing that native pronunciation is due to more forward tongue position, experimenting and monitoring output
           2. Matching specific forms of L1 to L2, then producing utterances to test for match

FIGURE 3.   Tactic Level of Processing

The makeup of the learner's filter is characterized by two features: (1) Constituents of the filter are not *processes* but do affect the selection of tactics responsible for obtaining data. For example, a learner who has a negative attitude toward speakers of the target language may prefer to use tactics which avoid face-to-face contact and rely instead on interaction with printed texts, tapes, etc., for obtaining needed data for the development of the target language grammar. (2) Some constituents of the filter would seem to be modifiable (semistatic or dynamic) while others appear to be unchanging (static).

Any change in the content of the filter may be assumed to have an effect on the selection of tactics. However, changes in the content of the filter would not affect the set of strategies, which is constant.

An example of a modifiable constituent of the filter would be motivation toward the target language. A learner may begin the process of L2 acquisition with the idea of simply learning enough language to enable him or her to function in university classes. Such a student has little patience or interest in developing social contacts with native speakers or in developing interpersonal communication skills. Such an attitude could lead to tactics limited to text-dependent learning, a focus on formal aspects of the language, and the desire to memorize vocabulary lists related to the student's special field of academic interest.

However, as we know, while a foreign student's initial motivation may be instrumental, it often changes as exposure to the target language and culture increases. A change in the type of motivation would also entail a change in the tactics employed to acquire the language. An integratively motivated student would use tactics which would bring him or her into contact with native speakers, and he or she would focus more on spoken forms of the language, since the student now senses a communicative function that the language can fulfill. It should be noted that both instrumental and integrative learners are capable of acquiring the language. It is not in the end result that they differ so much as in the tactics used to reach that end.

Since the view proposed by this model is that L2 acquisition is a subset of general learning in human beings, it is not surprising to find similarities between constituents of the L2 learner's filter and learner characteristics affecting first language acquisition. However, in spite of the fact that there are different types of L1 learners, all arrive at the same underlying system. These different types of L1 acquisition might also be described as different tactical styles. Bloom, Lightbown, and Hood (1978) found children who were imitators and those who were not. Peters (1977) describes analytic and gestalt learners. The gestalt learner relies more on imitation of phrases and routines, fewer nouns, and lots of pronouns. The analytic learner is the standard L1 acquirer who follows the route of two- or three-word sentences and increments in the MLU.

Birth order has been found to affect the manner of acquisition and the rate of acquisition. Nelson (1979) claimed that the type of L1 acquirer seemed to correspond to such factors as birth order and level of education and income of the home. Rosenblum and Dorman (1978) found that good imitators among 5- to 6-year-old subjects were either first-born or only children. It is not known whether these factors which affect first language acquisition also affect the style of second language acquisition.

One constituent of the filter which does change constantly is long-term memory. One definition of learning may be change which takes place in long-term memory, since learning, especially language learning, proceeds by building new structures on the basis of preexisting ones (Collins and Quillian 1972). Within *long-term memory* is stored all of the conceptual structures acquired by the learner up to the time of the current learning task. This would include both universal and language-specific grammars previously acquired by the learner. Since strategies form hypotheses by relating unknown entities to already acquired ones, each new acquisition changes the nature of long-term memory.

While long-term memory changes with each new acquisition, it in turn determines what is perceived from all the data to which the learner is exposed.

That is, long-term memory and its effect on the selection of tactics is what determines when input will become intake. Long-term memory acts as both a filter and a recipient of the act of acquisition. Because it determines how language data are perceived and therefore to what the learner becomes attuned, the filter may be said to *refract* strategies as they are given expression in performance as acquisition tactics.

For example, it may be hypothesized that different L1s cause learners to be attentive to different features of L2. In this sense, long-term memory in the filter affects cognitive function by causing the learner to tune in to certain features of L2 which also exist in L1. It would probably be more accurate to state that not just L1 but any other languages in the learner's long-term memory will affect the learner's perceptions of the target language data as well as have an effect on the selection of tactics which the learner chooses.

Rivers (1979) reports in diary form on her experiences learning Spanish as a sixth language. Two points of interest to the discussion at this juncture are that she reports that when learning vocabulary she followed the tactic of searching for cognates with French, her second language. She also reported that when she consciously tried to work out a sentence in Spanish she tended to think in German, her fourth langauge and probably the one she was least fluent in.

There is evidence that some languages even provide an advantage in terms of general cognitive development, as shown by an early study by Carroll (1964). In that research he showed that Navaho-speaking children performed a sorting task differently from English-speaking Navaho children. Children from English-speaking Navaho families sorted objects according to color while Navaho monolinguals sorted according to shape. Carroll's explanation for this finding was that the structure of Navaho requires the use of specific suffixes on the verb to denote the shape of the object used in conjunction with verbs of handling, giving, etc. Navaho children were thus sensitized to features of shape and size because the language required it.

Schachter and Rutherford (1979) suggest that not only the structure of the language but also its typology affect the output of the learner. In topic-prominent languages, a particular syntactic form is often tied to a specific discourse function. What learners of topic-prominent languages do is to assume that the same or similar relationship exists between syntactic form and discourse function in English and thus overproduce certain forms. Again it is a case of the content of the learner's long-term memory affecting his focus on the data in the second language. Knowledge stored in long-term memory affects how speakers of different languages realize strategies as tactics. Speakers of different first languages will apply strategies differently because of the different predetermined focus of the L1.

It was stated above that the content of long-term memory is constantly being changed with each new acquisition. Whether linguistic concepts related to language typology are in the same realm as other experiential knowledge and thus changeable remains a question for research. It may be that such knowledge will be modified as the learner matches and tests hypotheses about the nature of L2. That is, the cognitive set resulting from having acquired a language of contrasting typology might be amenable to change once contrasting hypotheses are tested. It would, however, require that the learner use tactics which would allow for such contrast or provide negative feedback for areas where positive transfer is mistakenly hypothesized.

THE ROLE OF THE LANGUAGE LEARNING ENVIRONMENT

While acquisition is dependent on the set of abstract, constant learning strategies, these strategies are manifested in the form of a behavioral response as tactics. As stated above, the degree to which tactics are outward context-specific realizations of the abstract characteristics of strategies is a function to a large degree of the learner's filter but also a function of what takes place outside the learner. Tactics are motivated by a response to the external environment.

In the strategy/tactic model, it is assumed that internal structures in the learner's filter decide what the learner perceives before any tactic can be activated. The degree to which a particular tactic may be said to be a *refraction* of an underlying strategy or simply a *reflection* of factors in the language learning environment will depend on the nature of factors in the learner's filter as well as features of the situation in which the acquisition act is taking place. Some learners appear to be controlled by or to conform to certain features in the environment while others develop subversive or supplementary tactics to overcome built-in weaknesses of the language learning environment. For example, given the normal second language classroom with many learners and one teacher model, some learners will engage both the teacher and other learners in informal conversations in order to receive more output and thus be enabled to test more hypotheses about the target language (Seliger 1983). Refractive tactics would be those related to underlying hypothesis-testing strategies while reflective tactics would consist of learner activity carried out to satisfy external demands without triggering an underlying strategic response in the form of hypothesis formation and testing. An example of such behavior would be the memorization and mechanical type of practice which is associated with audiolingual methodology. Such practice usually results in performance with little effect on underlying long-term competence when used without some communicative value.

Language learning tactics in the classroom would differ from tactics used outside the classroom because of the different demands of the two environ-ments. The classroom predisposes the learner to focus on form while naturalistic environments require predominantly a focus on content. In fact, classroom language learning may encourage the use of tactics which, while leading to formal analysis of linguistic form, interfere with the use of tactics which are more efficient for language learning or acquisition. A research question for the future is why the pseudo-learning brought about by the use of reflective tactics appeals to and satisfies some learners while others develop compensatory tactics which lead to real language acquisition.

CONCLUSIONS

This paper has argued that second language acquisition consists of two levels of processing: (1) processing which is independent of learner characteristics and learning context and universal to all language learning situations and (2) processing which is variable and specific to any given learner and context.

The first level of processing, strategy, is a biological, constant, learning process used by all human beings in all learning environments and consists of the abstract unconscious formulation of cognitive questions in the form of hypotheses attempting to relate new material to already established cognitive structures. The second level of processing, tactic, consists of specific responses in specific learning environments. Some tactics provide data from which strategies may derive underlying principles or rules of the language system while other tactics do not engage the hypothesis-formation process at the level of strategy. The selection of tactics is affected by both the language learning environment and the learner's filter, which determines what in the possible universe of language data is selected for attention and learning.

PART II

Affective Variables and Communicative Competence

4 Error Detection as a Function of Integrativity[1]

Jeff Kaplan and Michael Shand
San Diego State University

Unlike previous stiudies on the role of affective variables in second language acquisition (Spolsky 1969, Gardner and Lambert 1972, Schumann 1976, for example), which have focused on connections between psychological and/or social variables and overall success in second language acquisition, we will focus here on differences in the nature, rather than the degree, of the competence of second language learners as a function of affective variables. In particular, we will focus on connections between positive attitude toward a second language's culture and relative degree of acquisition of linguistic features as a function of the meaningfulness of the features. Briefly, our hypothesis is that a strongly integratively motivated second language learner (a "+I" learner) will be inclined to attend more to meaningful linguistic features than to nonmeaningful linguistic ones. Our hypothesis is based on the assumption that motivation that is integrative rather than nonintegrative results in the learner's having a greater concern with successful communication, i.e., with messages rather than with mere correctness of grammatical form. This assumption is plausible because, by definition, a +I learner wants to meet and interact socially with members of the second language culture, and meaningfulness is presumably even more important to successful social interaction than is correct grammar. That is, for a +I learner, "language is a means to an end rather than an end in itself" (Gardner and Lambert 1972, p.12).

An opposing hypothesis which might be maintained is that +I learners will want to speak and write as much as possible like native speakers of the L2, and as a result will be as concerned with grammatical form as with meaningfulness.

The results we will present here provide considerable support for the first hypothesis and provide little support for the second. That is, we have found data which suggest that +I learners do in fact unconsciously distinguish between more and less meaningful linguistic features to a greater extent than do learners who are low in integrative motivation.

To test these hypotheses, we first assessed second language learners' attitudes toward the second language culture—in this case, American culture—

as compared with their attitude toward their native culture. Learners who rated American culture higher than their native culture we assume to be integratively motivated learners (+I learners). This means of identifying integrative motivation is based on ideas proposed by Spolsky (1969). Second, we examine how integrative motivation affects performance in the second language.

METHOD

Two tasks were administered to 42 students enrolled in Linguistics 100 at San Diego State University, a course intended to improve the writing skills of nonnative speakers of English. Each student received a two-page questionnaire designed to measure his or her affective distance from, or "integrativity" with Americans and American culture (Appendix). Each student also received an error-detection task (to be described below).

Integrativity scores were assigned to each student on the basis of the questionnaire using a weighted measures procedure comparing how the student rated Americans relative to his or her native countrymen for those personal characteristics which the student considered most important.

Based on the integrativity scores, three groups of subjects were selected: those with high integrativity, those with low integrativity, and those whose integrativity score was near zero (for details, see Appendix). We will refer to subjects with high integrativity scores as "+I" learners, those with low integrativity scores as "−I" learners, and those whose integrativity score is near zero as "neutrals." Students who fell into any of these three groups but who correctly detected fewer than 20 errors on the error-detection task were removed from the groups because of the insufficient data they would provide. This admittedly somewhat arbitrary procedure yielded three groups of nine subjects each.

All the students were also administered a three-page error-detection task consisting of five narrative and descriptive texts. The texts contained errors of grammar and of meaning or logic. Subjects were instructed to circle as many errors as they could find. They were told that they would be given only 14 minutes for the task, and that reading quickly through the passages would enable them to catch the largest number of errors. A $5 bonus was promised to the subject in each class who correctly circled the largest number of errors. Baseline data for native speaker error-detection rates for the texts were obtained by administering the error-correction task to a group of 23 native speakers of English who were enrolled in an introductory linguistics course at San Diego State University. The native speaker subjects were given only 7 minutes for the task.

The error-detection passages contained 107 errors, including errors in each of the following categories: errors of meaning or logic (labeled L/S), errors of discourse tense agreement (DTA), omissions of redundant plural suffix (RPL), omissions of third person singular present tense -*s* (3 SG), and omissions of articles (ART). Examples of these are given in 1.

1   Examples of Error Types

L/S: Tim Perkins . . . was injured so badly that he was unable to play . . . *with Tim in the lineup*, our team was soundly defeated.

DTA: Before dawn on January 9, 1799, a remarkable creature came out of the woods . . . No one expected him. No one recognized him. He was human in bodily form and *walks* erect.

RPL: Variations in climate and geography account for many of these *contrast*.

3SG: Boston *contain* many stone paved streets that remind one of London.

ART: *Southeast*, though, presented a very different look and feel.

Students received scores for

Hits: number of errors they correctly detected

False alarms: number of correct items they mistakenly thought to be errors

Attempts: number of items they circled

Number of errors in each of the error categories they caught relative to the number of that type presented[2]

RESULTS

Fortuitously, after elimination of subjects who had fewer than 20 hits, the group proved to be closely matched in terms of the overall number of errors they correctly detected (hits). The +I learners correctly detected an average of 46.1 errors, the −I learners averaged 46.6 correct detections, and the neutrals averaged 44.6 correct detections. None of these averages differs significantly from any of the others [$F(2,8) = 0.20$, n.s.]. This is important for all the other results that follow, since if any of the groups were significantly better overall than the others, any between-groups differences which were found in any of the other measures could be attributed to differences in overall English proficiency for the different groups.

Comparison of the ratio of false alarms/attempts by group is shown in 2.

2

	+I	−I	N	E
False alarms				
Attempts	11.6%	29.1%	31.6%	12.5%

The +I subjects had a much lower ratio of *false alarms* to attempts than *neutrals* and −I subjects. The *neutrals* and −I learners attempted considerably more "corrections" than did the +I learners. However, as their *false alarm* rate was significantly higher than that of the +I learners, their overall performance in terms of the number of errors they caught (*hits*) was essentially no better than that of the +I learners. *T*-tests on these results show that the +I learners differ significantly from each of the other groups, while the other two groups do not differ significantly from each other (Table 1). *False alarm* rate for the native speaking subjects was 12.5 percent, which closely approximates the *false alarm* rate for the +I subjects.

Table 1. Comparison of *False Alarm* Rate by Subject Group

Comparison	t	p
+I / −I	10.46	<.001
+I / neutrals	9.39	<.001
−I / neutrals	1.27	n.s.

Error-detection rate by error type by subject group is shown in Table 2. The first four rows present the results from page 1 of the error-detection task. The second four rows present the results from pages 2 and 3 of the error-detection task. The data from page 1 and from pages 2 and 3 of the error-detection task are presented separately because the overall error-detection rate differed significantly for these sections, presumably reflecting differences in text difficulty.[3]

The meaning of the results summarized in Table 2 will become apparent when the error-detection rates that differ significantly from each other are singled out. These significant comparisons are presented in Tables 3A and 3B.

In Tables 3A and 3B, each > and < indicates that the detection rate of the two error types in question differed significantly by a *t*-test ($p<.05$).

Several noteworthy results emerge from these tables. First, 3SG was detected significantly more often than DTA and ART by all groups.

Second, on page 1 of the error-detection task, ART was detected less frequently by all groups than RPL and (as noted above) 3SG. However, when compared with DTA, there were no significant differences, except in the case of the +I group, where errors of DTA were detected significantly more often than ART errors.[4]

That 3SG should be detected not just frequently, but relatively more frequently than the DTA and ART errors, can perhaps be explained in terms of the relative saliency of the different error types. The high salience of 3SG errors could be due, first, to the relative closeness of the triggering element (the third person singular subject), and second, to the relative importance of the marked

Table 2. Error-Detection Rate by Error Type by Group

	3SG	RPL	DTA	ART	L/S
Page 1					
+I	.55	.43	.36	.07	
N	.52	.54	.26	.20	
−I	.49	.48	.24	.13	
E	.84	.65	.51	.46	
Page 2					
+I		.39	.60	.24	.49
N		.47	.64	.43	.51
−I		.56	.56	.47	.57
E		.63	.79	.64	.56

+I = integrative learners   −I = nonintegrative learners
N = neutral learners   E = native English speakers

Table 3A. Significant Differences in Error-Detection Rate by Error Type by Subject Group, Page 1

Error type comparison	+I	Neutral	−I	Natives
3SG–RPL				>
3SG–DTA	>	>	>	>
3SG–ART	>	>	>	>
RPL–DTA			>	
RPL–ART	>	>	>	>
DTA–ART	>			

Table 3B. Significant Differences in Error-Detection Rate by Error Type by Subject Group, Pages 2 and 3

Error type comparison	+I	Neutral	−I	Natives
RPL–DTA	< (tendency)			
RPL–ART				
DTA–ART	>			>
DTA–L/S				>
L/S–ART	>			
RPL–L/S				

> = first error type significantly greater than second (t-test, $p < .05$);
< = first error type lower than second.

word—verbs crucially determine aspects of sentence structure more than do members of other word classes. Further, a task of this type may tend to cause a subject to activate his or her explicit knowledge *about* the target language, and 3SG is very simple in terms of the knowledge required to respond appropriately. These factors operating singly or in conjunction with each other could account for this otherwise surprising finding.

An understanding of the results to be discussed below requires a brief discussion of differences in the level of meaningfulness among the error types. L/S errors, obviously, are high in meaningfulness. The other error types are redundant and predictable and are presumably lower in meaningfulness than L/S. In addition, DTA, RPL, and 3SG may each be argued to be higher on a meaningfulness scale than ART. With respect to DTA, a change in tense in a discourse is meaningful, although it may be contradictory. The same holds for a change in number on a noun following a quantifier. All examples of RPL in our data are of this sort. Similarly, for a third person singular suffix after a third person singular subject noun phrase, changing the verb inflection produces an incongruity. However, the absence of the omitted articles in the texts used in the present experiment does not result in any change of meaning; the only result is a loss of grammaticality. Thus, the first four examples in 1 are contradictory; the fifth is only ungrammatical. Errors in RPL and 3SG are grammatical errors (as might also be argued for DTA on a level of discourse grammar), but they are also semantically contradictory.

With respect to ii under 3, the relatively infrequent detection rate of ART errors can perhaps be understood in light of ART's relative lack of meaningfulness. Presumably, other things being equal, a feature relatively low in meaningfulness will tend to be relatively low in saliency. This tendency is most pronounced in the +I subjects. One reason for this may be that +I learners, more than other groups, seem to be attending to content, possibly resulting in less attention being directed to purely grammatical aspects of the task.[5]

Third, on pages 2 and 3 of the error-detection task, there was a tendency ($t = 1.59, p<.10$) for DTA errors to be detected more frequently than RPL errors by +I subjects (60 versus 39 percent). The error-detection rates did not differ significantly for *neutrals* or for −I subjects. This contrasts with page 1, where errors in RPL were detected more frequently than errors in DTA, although the difference reached significance only for the –I learners.

Fourth, comparison of L/S errors and ART errors for the three groups shows a significant difference only for the +I group, with L/S errors being detected significantly more often than ART errors.

These findings are summarized in 3.

3   i.   3SG was detected significantly more frequently than DTA and ART by all groups.
    ii. On page 1 of the error-detection task, all groups detected 3SG and RPL significantly more frequently than ART, but DTA > ART only for +I and native English subjects.
    iii. On pages 2 and 3 of the error-detection task, DTA > RPL for the +I subjects only. On page 1, errors in RPL > DTA.
    iv. L/S > ART for +I subjects only.

DISCUSSION

The significantly greater number of *attempts* on the part of the *neutrals* and −I's than on the part of the +I's, and the significantly lower ratio of *false alarms* to *attempts* on the part of the +I's when compared with the other groups (as shown in 2) may be attributable to a difference in tactics (Seliger 1982) between the +I subjects and members of the other groups when confronted with this type of error-detection task. *Neutrals* and –I subjects appear to have used relatively mechanical tactics on the error-detection task, devoting their attention, as instructed, primarily to a search for errors rather than to understanding the text. This focus on finding errors, together with their imperfect knowledge of English grammar, presumably caused them to erroneously circle many elements which were in fact correct. Conversely, the +I subjects appear to have attended to the communicative import of the text as well as to the assigned task of detecting errors. These subjects tended, therefore, to be accepting of a second language text as presented, catching errors only where the text conflicted jarringly with their knowledge of the language. Consequently, they tended to identify as errors primarily those items which were in fact errors.

We will now discuss in turn, each of the results listed in 3.

First, the high HIT rate for 3SG across groups is perhaps somewhat surprising. 3SG is of course notoriously absent in the spontaneous conversation of ESL learners. The high level of performance demonstrated on our error-detection task is perhaps best explained by noting the very different nature of an error-detection task as compared with spontaneous communicative second language production. Recognition requires a much lower level of competence than does production. This finding is compatible with the active involvement in a language task of this type of a grammatical monitor of the sort suggested by Krashen (1977).

With respect to iii under 3, an explanation is needed for the reversal in apparent relative degree of saliency of RPL and DTA on page 1 compared with pages 2 and 3. In general, other factors being equal, an error in a redundant feature whose trigger is relatively far away should be harder to detect compared with one whose trigger is relatively close, owing, at least in part, to differences in cognitive load at the level of short-term memory. This, however, interacts with (1) relative meaningfulness of the features, and (2) text difficulty. Apparently, as mentioned earlier, the texts on pages 2 and 3 of our error-detection task are easier to read than those on page 1. It makes sense, then, that on page 1, DTA errors would be detected relatively less frequently than RPL errors, since the text is relatively difficult and the triggers for DTA are all farther from the errors than are the triggers for RPL. On pages 2 and 3, on the other hand, where the texts are presumably easier, the negative effect of distance is attenuated. As a result, the error-detection rates for DTA are higher than on page 1.

With respect to iv, only the +I group shows a significant difference in error-detection rates for L/S errors and for ART errors. This can be attributed to the extreme difference in meaningfulness of the two error types together with the assumed greater attention to meaning on the part of the +I group in tasks of this kind. The +I subjects, being integratively motivated, may be more concerned with the meaningful aspects of a text than with mere correctness of grammatical form.

CONCLUSIONS

To summarize, we find that our data support the following conclusions:

1. Error saliency in a second language error-detection task seems to be affected by an interactive involvement of both meaningfulness and distance of a triggering element from a redundant linguistic feature.
2. Relative to nonintegrative learners, integrative learners are much more accepting of the second language, as shown by their strikingly lower *false alarm* rate. The reason for this may be that:
3. Integratively-motivated second language learners, when compared with non-integratively-motivated learners, are inclined to attend relatively more strongly to aspects of meaningfulness as opposed to aspects of grammar.

The last result suggests differences in second language tactics as a function of integrativity, and is compatible with the notion that semantic aspects of the message are relied upon more heavily by second language learners who are integratively motivated than by second language learners who are not integratively motivated.

Appendix.

Integrativity Questionnaire, page 1

DIRECTIONS: For each of the qualities below, how would you rate typical Americans? Circle the appropriate number, using the following scale:

1. Americans rate much higher in this quality than people from my home country.
2. Americans rate somewhat higher in this quality than people from home.
3. Americans and people from home are about equal in this quality.
4. People from my home country rate somewhat higher than Americans in this.
5. People from home rate much higher than Americans in this quality.

	Americans much higher	Americans somewhat higher	About equal	People from home somewhat higher	People from home much higher
Politeness	1	2	3	4	5
Honesty	1	2	3	4	5
Hard-workingness	1	2	3	4	5
Intelligence	1	2	3	4	5
Physical appearance	1	2	3	4	5
Religiousness	1	2	3	4	5
Sense of humor	1	2	3	4	5
Trustworthiness	1	2	3	4	5
Ability to tell jokes	1	2	3	4	5
Leadership	1	2	3	4	5
Friendliness	1	2	3	4	5
Sincerity	1	2	3	4	5

Integrativity Questionnaire, page 2

DIRECTIONS: How important are the following qualities in a friend? For each of the qualities below, indicate how important it is to you by circling a number on the scale from 1 (extremely important) to 5 (not important).

	Extremely important	Very important	Somewhat important	Rather unimportant	Not important
Politeness	1	2	3	4	5
Honesty	1	2	3	4	5
Hard-workingness	1	2	3	4	5
Intelligence	1	2	3	4	5
Physical appearance	1	2	3	4	5
Religiousness	1	2	3	4	5
Sense of humor	1	2	3	4	5
Trustworthiness	1	2	3	4	5
Ability to tell jokes	1	2	3	4	5
Leadership	1	2	3	4	5
Friendliness	1	2	3	4	5
Sincerity	1	2	3	4	5

NOTE: Only those traits which a student rated either "extremely important" (1) or "very important" (2) contributed to that student's integrativity score. Traits rated "extremely important" were doubly weighted, while those rated "very important" were weighted singly. This score was then multiplied by a weighted score for how the student felt Americans compared with his or her native countrymen. A weighting of $+2$ was assigned to those traits for which the student felt that Americans were "much higher" than people from his or her native country. $+1$ was assigned where Americans were rated "somewhat higher," 0 was assigned where the rating "about the same" was given, -1 for "Americans somewhat lower," and -2 for "Americans much lower." Thus, if a student rated "honesty" as "extremely important" and rated Americans "much lower," a -4 (2×-2) was added to his or her integrativity score for that trait. By summing up the scores from all the characteristics which the subject rated either "extremely important" or "very important," a measure of integrativity was obtained.

Three groups of subjects were selected based on these questionnaires: those with high integrativity (defined post hoc as a score of $+5$ or higher), those with low integrativity scores (defined as a score of -5 or lower), and those whose integrativity score was near zero (defined as a score of $+1$, 0, or -1 on the questionnaire).

NOTES

1. We would like to thank Zev Bar-Lev, Tom Donahue, Gabriella Hermon, Philip Hubbard, and Phyllis King for allowing us class time to conduct our experiment, and we would like to thank their students for serving as subjects. This work was supported in part by National Science Foundation Grant BNS 79-01670 to Jeffrey L. Elman, University of California, San Diego.

2. Not all students completed the task. Students were assumed to have been presented with all occurrences of all five error types up to the point of their last attempt.

3. Error-detection rate (*hits/attempts*) for page 1 and pages 2 and 3 of the error-detection task:

Group	Page 1 %	Pages 2, 3 %	t =	p <
$+I$	82.22	90.87	1.49	.10
$-I$	54.89	76.00	2.54	.02
Neutral	62.56	74.33	2.19	.05
Groups combined	66.56	80.37	3.78	.001

4. Error-detection rate for RPL errors was significantly higher than for DTA errors. We offer no explanation for this. However, the correlation between saliency and meaningfulness of error type, which we discuss below, does not hold here, since RPL and DTA seem to be more or less equal in meaningfulness.

5. It is doubtful that the lower detection rate for article errors by the $+I$ subjects is attributable to the presence or absence of articles in the subjects' first language, since for each subject group, an equal number of subjects spoke native languages which have articles.

5 Communicative Tactics in Children's Second Language Acquisition

Muriel Saville-Troike, Erica McClure, and Mary Fritz
University of Illinois at Urbana-Champaign

Children who have developed communicative competence in their first language have already acquired strategies for engaging others in interaction, for asking and giving relevant information, for cooperating in conversations, and for expressing wants and needs. Second language acquisition is largely a matter of learning new linguistic forms to fulfill the same functions within a different social milieu.

Although the focus in second language research has shifted from the attainment of grammatical competence to the acquisition of communicative competence, there have still been very few studies which have examined either the development of communicative forms in a naturalistic setting or the nature of the communicative tactics that children use with one another while they are still in the early stages of second language development and have limited linguistic means at their disposal.

Our research, which is ethnographic in nature, addresses the following questions: What do children in this situation need to accomplish in various communicative contexts during the first weeks and months in the United States? What tactics do they use to fulfill these functions, and how do these develop through the year? What is the relative effectiveness of different tactics for accomplishing the children's intent? Are there systematic differences either in children's communicative needs or in their tactics which might be attributable to native language background, social circumstances, or personality factors? By "communicative tactics" we mean what linguistic or nonlinguistic means at their disposal the children select to try to accomplish their communicative goal.

METHOD

The population for our research consisted of 20 speakers of Japanese, Korean, Hebrew, Spanish, Icelandic, and Polish who were enrolled in a multilingual program in the Urbana, Illinois, public schools. In this elementary school, 41 percent of the students were native speakers of a language other than English, and all native English-speaking students were required to study a foreign language.

The children in our sample ranged in age from 7 to 12 years, with concentrations at ages 7 and 9 (grades 2 and 4). At the time of their selection at the beginning of the fall semester, all the subjects (1) knew very little or no English, (2) were already literate in their native languages, and (3) had well-educated parents (professors or graduate students at the University of Illinois).

The 20 children were divided into two groups for daily 30-minute pull-out ESL instructional periods, according to their age and maturity level. We videotaped these sessions once a week throughout the 1981–1982 school year, and also audiotaped the first 10 minutes of each session another two times a week. Additionally, we observed weekly in regular classrooms and in other school contexts, videotaped once a month in regular classrooms, and audio-taped and videotaped irregularly in other situations (e.g., on the playground, in the library and halls, and in native language reading sessions).

The quantitative data presented in Tables 1 to 3 are derived from a total of 8 hours of videotaping: the first 4 hours filmed in the ESL pull-out situation in September and early October, and the seventeenth through twentieth hours filmed in January and early February.

Videotapes were scripted and checked by four researchers; all communicative acts in each sequence were then coded for inferred speaker intent, using a system adapted from Dore (1978).

SITUATION AND EVENTS

The ESL sessions divided themselves into a regular sequence of events. These are listed below, together with the number of children's communicative acts occurring in each event during the 8 hours of filming used for this sample:

	No. of acts	
	Sept.	Jan.
1. Unstructured/child-directed	144	113
2. "Claiming a seat"	39	36
3. Teacher-directed discussion (e.g., "Where's Peter?")	35	131
4. Opening routines (e.g., "What day is it today?")	36	11
5. Teacher-directed lesson or activity	88	281
6. Explanation of follow-up activity	59	94
7. Follow-up activity	159	153
8. Closing	38	84

We call the first event in each session "unstructured" or "child-directed." As part of the research design, but also occurring naturally in previous years, the children were left alone without adult supervision or intervention before the ESL teacher came into the room and called them to the instructional area. When she did, they had an event we call "claiming a seat," during which the children challenged, claimed, and negotiated for their favorite position at a single large table. During these two events, almost all communication that took place was between children.

Table 1 indicates the percentage of acts within each event the children addressed to other children (from same and different native language background) and to the teacher. Unlike the first two events, events 3, 4, 5, and 8 are teacher-directed, and almost all of the children's communicative acts in those events are addressed to her. Events 6 and 7 are less structured, usually including an art project or game, and children address each other as well as the teacher. Since we wish to focus primarily on child-child communication for this part of our analysis, our examples for this report are drawn from the first, second, and seventh segments of the sessions.

Table 1.

Addressee	(% within each event)							
Child: Same L	29.6	6.7	8.4	2.1	.3	12.4	19.2	2.5
Child: Dif L	65.4	89.3	8.4	6.4	5.1	10.5	31.1	8.2
Teacher	2.7	4.0	83.1	91.5	91.1	76.5	50.6	81.1
Other	1.9	0	0	0	.2	.7	0	8.2

COMMUNICATIVE FUNCTIONS

The system for coding speech acts that was devised by Dore (1978) includes categories of requests, responses to requests, descriptions of facts, statements of rules and beliefs, acknowledgments which recognize and evaluate responses and nonrequests, organization devices that regulate contact and conversation, and performatives. Our most significant modification was in extending the system to include nonverbal as well as verbal communicative acts; additionally, we have added request and response types for vocabulary identification, repetition, and expansion (e.g., "Use a complete sentence"), and new categories for translation and interaction (e.g., invitation, acceptance, and rejection of interaction, display behavior, and phatic communication with no propositional content).

As can be seen in Table 2, the first two events in each session include a much higher percentage of interactional and performative acts than do the events which are primarily directed by the teacher. The most common of the former are moves which are entries into interaction and the following acceptance or rejection by another child, or interaction which involves only phatic communication. The most common performatives are teasing, claims, and protests. Almost all requests and responses in these first two events are for action, to do or stop doing something, rather than for information or clarification.

Table 2.

Communicative functions	(% within each event)							
	1	2	3	4	5	6	7	8
September:								
Requests	20.1	10.3	25.7	5.6	5.7	18.6	17.6	13.2
Responses	13.2	23.1	28.6	63.9	51.1	45.8	31.4	26.3
Descriptions	12.5	0	5.7	0	12.5	28.8	8.8	7.9
Statements	3.5	2.6	8.6	0	0	3.4	3.8	0
Acknowledgments	5.6	0	0	5.6	0	10.2	3.8	13.2
Org. devices	6.3	5.1	2.9	8.3	25.0	32.2	10.7	0
Interactional	22.2	20.5	5.7	8.3	1.1	10.2	4.4	36.8
Performatives	15.3	38.5	5.7	8.3	1.1	5.1	14.5	2.6
Exclamations	1.4	0	14.3	0	2.3	5.1	2.5	2.6
January:								
Requests	11.5	22.2	17.6	0	9.6	17.0	24.2	21.4
Responses	4.4	13.9	31.3	54.5	34.9	7.4	23.5	22.6
Descriptions	14.2	0	18.3	0	24.2	17.0	9.8	7.1
Statements	5.3	0	1.5	0	.7	5.3	12.8	2.4
Acknowledgments	0	0	8.4	45.5	2.8	1.1	4.6	7.1
Org. devices	0	0	6.1	0	13.2	23.4	2.6	7.1
Interactional	31.9	5.6	4.6	0	.7	2.1	1.3	17.9
Performatives	29.2	13.9	7.6	0	10.7	10.6	17.6	11.9
Exclamations	3.5	5.6	4.6	0	1.8	9.6	8.5	1.2

Looking at developmental differences across all events during the 4-month period represented, there was a drop in questions requiring a yes/no answer, and a rise in wh-, action, and identification questions. Children also made many more requests to check their own understanding as time went on, both in English and in their native languages.

Responses showed an even more significant change in type: for example, where 50 percent of responses were repetitions or memorized recitation in September, fewer than 13 percent were by January; on the other hand yes/no responses climbed from 8 to 20 percent, and wh-responses from 0.5 to 16 percent of responses in that category.

There was little change in the quantity of interactional acts during this period, but more invitations were issued for interaction in January as opposed to children entering interaction without some kind of invitation. Perhaps for this reason, the rejection rate was much lower by the middle of the school year.

Teasing dropped from 40 to 11 percent of performative acts, and the number of warnings also declined. Contrary to our expectations, occurrence of sound play quadrupled, perhaps because it proved to be such an enjoyable and successful interactional activity. Its form changed, however, from play primarily based on other children's names to nonspeech sounds. Joking was introduced late in the period under investigation, taking both nonverbal and verbal forms.

COMMUNICATIVE FORM

A relatively high percentage of functions in the first two events was accomplished nonverbally, as can be seen in Table 3, and there was a significant drop in native language use as English developed as a lingua franca.

It is of interest that teasing was still limited almost entirely to nonverbal behavior and the speaker's native language. By January, however, and when rejection of interaction occurred at midyear, it was still nonverbal: e.g., children turned their backs on one another.

Statements and descriptions were still not common functions in the children's communication by January but were increasing. The only frequent type of description expressed in English in September was mere identification or labeling, with 70 percent of the description of events or properties expressed nonverbally or in the speaker's native language, but 64 percent of even these subtypes were expressed in English by January.

Table 3.

Communicative forms	(% used for each function)					
	N	L1	ER	EW	EM	O
September:						
Requests	21.7	28.3	15.2	19.6	14.1	1.1
Responses	23.8	2.3	15.7	44.8	20.9	4.1
Descriptions	9.4	23.4	9.4	43.8	12.5	0
Statements	11.1	72.2	0	0	16.7	0
Acknowledgments	18.5	0	18.5	22.2	7.4	33.3
Org. devices	36.1	9.7	15.3	11.1	0	29.2
Interactional	50.0	7.8	35.9	1.6	1.6	3.1
Performatives	36.0	16.0	28.0	9.3	1.3	8.0
Exclamations	5.6	16.7	16.7	0	0	61.1
January:						
Requests	21.8	10.9	14.3	16.8	34.5	0
Responses	19.9	1.2	21.1	44.0	10.2	2.4
Descriptions	17.3	5.1	1.5	33.1	40.6	2.3
Statements	0	21.7	21.7	26.1	30.4	0
Acknowledgments	12.0	12.0	40.0	4.0	12.0	20.0
Org. devices	40.0	0	8.0	26.7	5.3	20.0
Interactional	40.7	5.1	39.0	8.5	1.7	1.7
Performatives	37.3	3.7	9.1	6.4	24.5	19.1
Exclamations	26.5	2.9	2.9	0	17.6	50.0

N = nonvocal (e.g., gesture, facial expression; not counted if an accompaniment of speech)
L1 = native language
ER = English: routine (e.g., shut up, bye-bye)
EW = English: single word
EM = English: more than one word
O = other vocalization (e.g., Oh!, Ah!, nonspeech sound)

CONVERSATIONS

The following episode occurred on the first day of videotaping in September and illustrates the earliest tactics that our subjects used to converse with one another. As it began, three children were seated at a table: K1 (a Korean boy), J1 (a Japanese boy), and J3 (a Japanese girl). J1 and K1 exchanged a politeness routine to indicate the conversation.

J1	>	K1	EXCUSE ME.
K1	>	J1	EXCUSE ME.
J1	>	K1	EXCUSE ME.

K1 needed something new to say. Cards with colors and shapes had been left on the table, the vocabulary that had been presented thus far in ESL. K1 picked one up and named it. J3 joined the conversation, naming a color, and J1 repeated "Excuso."

K1	TRAYHANGLE.	
J3	RET.	"Red."
J1	EXCUSO.	

Conversation continued, with the children making use of the questioning/ testing/correction procedures learned in ESL as well as the vocabulary presented there. Since they were enrolled in different regular classrooms, ESL was the only language learning experience they had in common.

K1	>	J3	Shows her a picture.
J3	>	K1	LADY. Pronounced /ladi/, with low-mid a.
K1	>	J3	LADY. Pronounced /leydi/, correcting her pronunciation.
			NO /LADI/ . . . /LEYDI/.

They proceeded to more substantive discussion, with the children success-fully using a single referential term, brand name, or simple phrase (e.g., television, RCA, Japan Sony) for asking questions, making statements about the nature of the video equipment, and finally negotiating agreement that the make was RCA. J3 unsuccessfully tried to use Japanese with a Korean speaker.

K1	>	J3	TELEVISION?
J3	>	K1	[Japanese: "No it's not."]
J1	>	J3	[Japanese: "It's . . . a . . ."] RADIO.
J3	>	K1	RADIO?
K1	>	J3	COLOR TELEVISION.
			RCA?
			NO?
			SONY?
			WHAT KIND JAPAN SONY?
J3	>	K1	WHAT?
K1	>	J3	JAPAN SONY?
			TELEVISION.
J3	>	K1	WHAT?
K1	>	J3	TELEVISION!

J3	>	K1	TELEVISION?
K1	>	J3	YA! YA! TELEVISION.
K1	>	J1	JAPAN SONY.
J1	>	K1	SONY.
J1	>	K1	RCA?
			NO?
K1	>	J1	RCA.

Four other children joined the group: one Korean boy (K2), one Japanese boy (J2), and two Japanese girls (J4 and J5). K1 and K2 interacted with the girls in sound play based on the girls' names, and J5 responded nonverbally.

K2	>	J3	AKIKU, KIKU, KIKU. Sound play.
K1	>	J3	KIKU KU, KU, KU, KU.
K2	>	J5	OK. HEY.
J5	>	K1	Waves her sweater at him.
K1	>	J5	KA-RU. KA-RU.
J5			Fiddles more with her sweater.

K1 continued with one of the few phrases he knew in Japanese, although it was meaningless in this context.

K1	>	J5	[J: KARU, KEKKO KEKKO, KEKKO DESU "Karu, no, no thank you."]

The children continued their interaction with a Korean boy teasing that Japanese are "cracked" (crazy), and more sound play.

K2	>	J4	JAPANESE.
			JAPANESE KRAKU.
K2	>	J1	[Korean: DOGINO HAKTTAK, HUKTTAK.]
			Sound play (like Japanese clock; Koreans use different sounds to indicate "ethnicity" of clocks, including /ng/ for American clock, etc.) Korean children understand the sounds DO, NO, GI, DA, MO as representing Japanese.
K2	>	J1	[Korean: DOGNINO HAKTTAK, HUKTTAK.]
J1	>	K2	Smiles.
K2	>	J2	JAPANESE KRAKU.
			Points toward J4.
			[Korean: adds explanation]
J2	>	K2	Laughs.
K2	>	J3	AKIKU, KIKU, KIKU.

The second episode occurred two weeks later as Japanese (J6), Korean (K4), and Spanish (S1) speaking boys worked together to assemble a puzzle map of the world. Conversational rounds consisted mainly of one child naming a referent and the other children taking turns repeating the term in round robin fashion.

S1			AMERICA.
			Finds puzzle piece of the United States and puts it in place.
J6	>	S1	Picks up his hand and moves it out of the way.
J6			JAPANI, JAPANI.
			Points to place in puzzle frame where the Japan piece will go.
K4			JAPANI.
S1			JAPANI.

J6		JAPANI.
S1		JAPANI.
J6		AH. JAPANI. Finds Japan piece to puzzle.
		KOREA. Also claims to have found Korea.

Adding only "No," and using different stress and intonation contours, the children disagreed and questioned one another.

K4	>	J6	NO KOREA.
J6	>	K4	KOREA.
K4	>	J6	NO.
J6	>	K4	KOREA.
S1	>	J6	KOREA?
K4	>	S1	NO.
S1	>	K4	[Spanish: SI?]

K4 offered an explanation, which the others acknowledged by repeating it after him.

K4	>	S1	YES, YES, YES.
			NO KOREA.
			PINK KOREA. (Stress on "pink.")
			"Pink" refers to the color of the Korean map piece; i.e., "It can't be Korea, because Korea is pink."
J6			PINK.
S1			PINK.
K4			KOREA. Finds piece and puts it in place.

Interaction continued with physical contact and speech play.

S1	>	K4	Taps him on arm.
K4	>	S1	Looks at him.
J6	>	S1	Takes a swipe at him.
S1	>	J6	Returns the swipe.
J6	>	S1	OMADA, OMADA, OMADA.
			Japanese prefix O- "big," as in "Omar," a play on S1's name.

The ESL teacher (T2) entered the scene, telling the class (CL) it was time to clean up. K4 unsuccessfully tried to protest to the teacher in Korean, and a Hebrew speaking girl (H2) repeated the teacher's routine "Time to stop" in a teasing manner to him.

T2	>	CL	OK, TIME TO STOP.
T2	>	CL	PUT AWAY THE GAME, PLEASE.
K4	>	T2	Points to puzzle.
			[Korean: "Ah! I have to finish."]
T2	>	CL	TIME TO STOP. (Rising intonation)
H2	>	K4	TIME TO STOP. (Imitates T's intonation)
K4	>	H2	Looks at her (threateningly).

This sequence concluded with more repetition and nonverbal tactics, including the teacher's nonverbal control measures. The most complex English structure occurred when K4 told J6 he should walk instead of run. J6's very negative response to K4 was in Japanese.

T2 > CL	AND LET'S SIT AT THE TABLE.
J6	TABLE.
K4	TABLE.
J6 and K4	Leap up and run toward table.
T2 > K4	Grabs him with arm around neck and shoulder.
K4 > T2	HE.
	Points toward table.
	Protesting that J6 got away with running to claim chair.
K4 > J6	HEY, WALKING.
J6 > K4	[J: DAMARE! "Shut up"]

It is apparent that from the beginning these children have conversational skills for attention getting and turn taking, and relate their moves in a coherent manner to the form and content of the one that precedes it. In Grice's (1975) terms, they know the cooperative principle of conversation, and are "relevant." The earliest communicative forms available to these children (as for children acquiring a first language) are nonvocal behaviors, sound play and nonspeech sounds, simple routines, repetition of part or all of previous utterances, and single referential terms they are beginning to learn in English (cf. Keenan 1974, Peck 1978). Additionally, these second language learners have access to first language forms and tactics, and have had experience interacting with other children.

All the children who participated in conversations with other children early in the year made use of the same tactics, no matter what their native language background. It is important to note, however, that not all the children engaged in intragroup social interaction. It is not possible to separate cultural and personality factors in determining why some did not, but those who did not were children who appeared either to be less aggressive or to hold themselves aloof.

NARRATIVES

Unlike early conversational tactics, children used basically different means for describing events and actions during the early stages of learning English. One tactic was to use a single lexical term (usually the name of the topic the child wanted to convey information about). Completion of the proposition required a cooperative addressee, who asked one or more questions that allowed the child to respond with a simple "yes" or "no." This tactic was used more frequently with adults than with other children.

The following sequence, which exemplifies this tactic, was in response to a teacher's (T1) question about why another child had not come to class.

J6 > T1	PICTURE.
T1 > J6	SHE'S MAKING A PICTURE?
J6 > T1	YES.
T1 > J6	WILL SHE COME WHEN SHE'S FINISHED?
J6 > T1	YES.

The same cooperative process continued for the construction of longer texts even after children could express a whole proposition themselves by stringing together multiple terms in English, with adults first providing expanded models, and later prompting expansions by asking wh- questions. This rarely occurred in child-child communication, and never between limited English speakers.

The second tactic was to create a complete topic-comment proposition by using both verbal and nonverbal means, usually naming the topic in English and then providing a nonverbal comment, sometimes accompanied by verbalization in the native language.

In the following example K4 named both agent and object as he communicated to the teacher (T2) that Taki (J6) had thrown a pencil at him while passing out supplies.

K4 >	T2	TEACHER. TEACHER.
T2 >	K4	Goes over to him.
K4 >	T2	TAKI.
		PENCIL.
		Makes throwing motion.
		TAKI.
		UN . . . HE.
		Makes throwing motion again.
T2 >	J6	TAKI,
		PLEASE DON'T THROW PENCILS.

Most children used this tactic more frequently with other children than with adults, but a few used it almost exclusively for any situation.

The general preference for a nonverbal mode of description to children and verbal to adults is illustrated in the following sequence. A Korean boy (K1) has hit his younger brother (K2). The event is reported nonverbally to an Icelandic girl (I1), and then verbally to the teacher (T1).

I1 >	J1	WHAT HAPPEN?
J3 >	I1	Arms in circle; pulls down.
J1 >	I1	Punches fist into own palm.
		Both indicating K2 was hit.
J3 >	T1	Goes over to where T is in table area.
		TEACHER.
		K . . . CRYING.

The final example illustrates how the tactic of combining verbal and nonverbal components developed into longer narrative structures. The teacher (T2) has just returned snowmen the children had made out of popcorn, and they were going to take them home on the bus. K4 addressed the following narrative to the teacher, but he was also performing for the entire class.

K4 >	T2	JUST SAW ME.
		JUST SAW ME.
		i.e., "Look at me"; using "saw" for "see."
		THIS IS BUS.
		Moves two chairs side by side to make bus seats.

ONE.
Slaps one seat.
THIS IS ONE.
THIS IS YOUR BUS.
THIS IS BUS.
DULKUNG DULKUNG.
Means jolting of bus.
Thrusts arms out in front.
SNOWMAN LIKE THAT.
Holds hands palm up in front.
[T has shown children how to hold snowmen "like a baby" so that the popcorn won't fall off.]
RIGHT HERE FRIENDS. (Calls, with circus barker quality. Addressing imaginary audience on bus.)
Points beside him.
HERE SNOWMAN.
YUM.
Mimes eating.
EAT THEM.

T2 > K4   YOU TELL YOUR FRIENDS, "DO NOT EAT MY SNOWMAN." OK?
K4 > T2   JUST SAW ME.
           MY CLASS EAT THEM.
T2 > K4   YOU TELL YOUR CLASS NOT TO EAT THEM.

The general pattern for such longer narratives by children who preferred this tactic was: (1) getting attention (e.g., "just saw me"), (2) indicating focus (e.g., "this," "right here," tapping the object that was in focus), (3) naming objects, and (4) acting out the event.

CONCLUSIONS

By the end of the school year the 20 subjects differed greatly in the degree to which they had mastered English, and their level of accomplishment in reading and other subjects taught through the medium of English. Our analysis of the data is not complete, but the narrative and conversational patterns children select appear to be systematically related to their success in learning English.

Our data suggest the existence of two basic narrative patterns. Children were almost equally divided at the beginning of the year in their preference for using a "stringing" tactic for developing narrative or a "holistic" tactic (i.e., using whole messages from the beginning, even when they required a combination of English routines, native language, gestures, nonspeech sounds, and drawing pictures). Some in each group progressed to fairly complex English structures during the course of the year, and some in each group did not, but the "stringers" had more early success communicating with adults and the whole message users with other children. The "stringers" have also in general met with more success in transferring their reading skills to English.

We have already reported the apparent universality of early conversational tactics for children who interact socially with one another. However, a few of our subjects rarely spoke to the other children during the ESL sessions that were audio and videotaped. Even in their regular classrooms and on the playground, they appeared to make minimal use of their developing English for social purposes.

Here we report a counteruniversal. It has been claimed by Wong-Fillmore (1976) that such social contact is a critical and necessary factor in second language development. While some of our subjects fit her description, it does not hold true with greater numbers of children and a greater variety of native languages and cultures. In fact, the *least* sociable of our subjects include those who have acquired the most English vocabulary and grammar during this period, and who have achieved best in content areas of the curriculum taught through English. We have heard children who used virtually no language at all in a group context for 2 to 3 months suddenly begin to speak complex English sentences. However, two other children who did not engage in much verbal interaction with the others proved to be among the poorest in their language development; so we are not suggesting any simple correlation, and certainly no cause-effect relationship. A striking observation, nevertheless, is that some of the more successful communicators, at least in the contexts we recorded, have fossilized at fairly early levels of development, their very success seeming to have reduced their motivation to learn more complex linguistic forms. This fossilization is particularly evident among those who have continued to combine verbal and nonverbal actions to express propositions.

These findings have major relevance for research methodology. First, focusing data collection on only the verbal content of a proposition misses a major dimension of communicative phenomena. Furthermore, although recent focus on the development of communicative competence is an important and necessary direction for both research and pedagogy to take, it is not sufficient. Second language learning for children has more complex dimensions when it is a language through which they must learn to learn, as well as a medium for social interaction.

PART III

Interlanguage Studies

A. Comparisons With
First Language Acquisition

6 A Universal in L2 Acquisition Based on a PBD Typology[1]

Suzanne Flynn
Massachusetts Institute of Technology

This paper reports the results of an experimental study of adult second language acquisition which provides evidence that a typology based on the "principal branching direction" (PBD) of a learner's first language will significantly predict certain aspects of a second language learner's processing and acquisition of complex sentence structures. Results indicate that second language learners are sensitive to differences in the PBD of the first and second language, and that they use this sensitivity to develop various structural aspects of the second language, specifically grammatical anaphora. Where the first and second language match in PBD, processing and acquisition of complex sentences are facilitated. Where the first and second language do not match in PBD, processing is disrupted and acquisition is delayed.

Branching direction (BD) is generally defined (Chomsky 1964) as follows:

1. *Right-branching structure* reflects the generation of recursive terms to the right of a nonnull site (i.e., $A \rightarrow \alpha A$, where α represents some nonnull site) (cf. Chomsky 1964, p. 123, fn. 9).
2. *Left-branching structure* reflects the generation of recursive terms to the left of a nonnull site (i.e., $A \rightarrow A \alpha$).

Principal branching direction (PBD) (Lust 1983) is evaluated with regard to major recursive devices of a language, e.g., relative clause, adverbial subordinate clause, and sentence complementation. For example, in a language where the PBD is *right,* each structure in the set of major recursive devices will be right-branching.

In general, BD refers to the direction, right or left, in which major recursive devices, such as relative clauses or other forms of sentence complementation, can be generated in relation to a head.[2] Sentences 1 to 4 exemplify this principle for English and Spanish, which are considered to be principally right-branching languages, and sentences 5 and 6 exemplify this principle for Japanese, which is principally left-branching.

Right-Branching PBD

English
Relative Clause:

1   This is the book that the man I met on the train going to Tokyo wrote.

Subordinate Adverbial Clause:

2   John plays chess when smoking his pipe.

Spanish
Relative Clause:

3   La novela que escribió es muy original. (The book that wrote (third singular past) is very original.) "The book that he wrote is very original."

Subordinate Averbial Clause:

4   Escucharé música mientras leo el manuscrito. (Listen (first singular future) music while read (first singular present) the manuscript.) "I will listen to music while I read the manuscript."

Left-Branching PBD

Japanese
Relative Clause:

5   [Kore wa [[[Tokyo e iku] kisha de atta] otoko no hito no kaita] hon desu] (this Tokyo to go train met man wrote book is) "This is the book that the man I met on the train going to Tokyo wrote." (See Smith 1978)

Subordinate Clause:

6   [[Uchi ni kaetta t ki] rumeto ga pati O shite ita] (home to returned time roommate party doing was) "When I returned home, my roommate was having a party."

Experimental first language acquisition studies which have compared English, Arabic, Japanese, and Chinese children's early acquisition of complex sentence structures have shown that a typology based on the PBD of a child's first language significantly predicts early patterns of acquisition of complex sentence structures such as those shown in 7 to 12. Results of first language acquisition studies have shown that children are sensitive to the PBD of their first language and use this sensitivity to construct hypotheses about a critical aspect of the grammar of their first language, namely, grammatical anaphora (Lust 1981; Lust and Wakayama 1979; Lust, Loveland, and Kornet 1980; Lust and Chien 1980; Lust and Barazangi ms.; Lust, Solan, Flynn, Cross, and Schuetz 1981).

Principle of First Language Acquisition

In early child language, direction of grammatical anaphora accords with the principal branching direction of the specific language being learned (Lust 1981).

For example, English-speaking children have been found to prefer sentences with *forward* anaphora in accord with the *right*-branching structure of English. That is, they prefer forward anaphora exemplified in sentences 7 and 9 but eschew backward anaphora as in sentences 8 and 10. On the other hand, Japanese-speaking children have been found to prefer backward anaphora as in 12, rather than sentences with forward anaphora as in 11. This preference for backward anaphora by Japanese children accords with the left-branching structure of Japanese.

Experimental work is now being conducted to test this hypothesis of PBD in relation to children's first language acquisition of subordinate clauses in several languages.

First Language Acquisition Data

English
Coordination:

7   Forward: *Dogs* bark and Ø bite.

8   Backward: Birds Ø and crickets *sing*.

Subordination:
9   Forward: *Oscar* bumped the wall when *he* found the penny.

10   Backward: When *he* closed the box, *Kermit* lay down.

Japanese
Coordination:

11   Forward: *Inu wa* hoeru shi Ø kamit suku.

                        "*Dogs* bark and Ø bite."
12   Backward: Tori Ø to mushi wa *naku*.

                        "Bird Ø and cricket *sing*."

If first language acquisition findings continue to confirm the principle of first language acquisition, these data will provide evidence that children's sensitivity to the PBD of their first language is a significant principle in first language acquisition. This principle provides a significant constraint on children's early development of critical aspects of their first language grammar, one such aspect being anaphora.

IMPLICATIONS FOR ADULT SECOND LANGUAGE ACQUISITION

The study reported here tested two related questions: whether the sensitivity specified by the PBD typology which was evidenced in first language acquisition would also be evidenced in adult second language acquisition and, more particularly, whether this sensitivity would provide a constraint on the acquisition of anaphora in second language acquisition, as it had in first. It was hypothesized that if sensitivity to the PBD is a significant part of the essential language faculty and if acquisition of a second language involves this essential language faculty, then second language acquisition should involve this principle of PBD in some way. Specifically, if a learner's hypotheses about PBD are necessary to the acquisition of the second language as well as to the first, then we would expect that there would be significantly more difficulty in second language acquisition where there is a mismatch between the PBD of the first and second languages and less difficulty where there is not a PBD mismatch. One might expect that hypotheses of adult second language learners about branching direction are set for first the first language and would need to be revised if the PBD of the second language differs from that of the first. However, no such revision in hypotheses would be necessary where the first and second languages match in PBD.

Moreover, if these hypotheses about PBD constrain the acquisition of anaphora, we would predict that the first and second language PBD mismatch would affect the acquisition of anaphora in particular. Specifically, we would predict more anaphora errors particularly with regard to directionality of anaphora where the first language does not match the second language in PBD given the principle of first language acquisition. Where the PBD of the second language matches that of the first language, one might expect the pattern of acquisition of anaphora in the second language acquisition process to be similar to that in the first, but one would not necessarily predict this where there was a PBD mismatch.

These predictions are summarized in the following experimental hypotheses:

1. Acquisition of complex sentence structures will differ significantly between (L1 PBD=L2 PBD) vs. (L1 PBD≠L2 PBD). Acquisition will be superior where L1 PBD=L2 PBD.

2. Processing of complex sentences during early stages of L2 acquisition will differ significantly between (L1 PBD=L2 PBD) vs. (L1 PBD≠L1 PBD). L2 acquisition patterns will be similar to L1 acquisition patterns where L1 PBD =L2 PBD, but not necessarily where L1 PBD≠L2 PBD.

EXPERIMENTAL STUDY

For this study two groups of adult Ss studying English as a second language in this country were tested. One group consisted of 51 Ss whose first language was Spanish, principally a right-branching language like English, and the second group consisted of 53 Ss whose first language was Japanese, principally a left-branching language unlike English or Spanish. The mean age for the Spanish-speaking Ss was 24 years, while that of the Japanese Ss was 30 years.

All *S*s were tested on a set of complex sentences with pre- and postposed subordinate adverbial clauses both with and without pronominal anaphoras which varied in direction.

Prior to the experimental testing, all *S*s were administered a standardized ESL proficiency test, the *English Placement Test* from the University of Michigan. Based on the results of this test, *S*s were placed into one of the three levels of English ability, beginning, intermediate, and advanced. The listening comprehension and grammar subtests of the Placement Test were selected to determine the ESL proficiency level of each *S*. Results shown in Table 1 indicate that the two language groups were comparable in terms of ESL proficiency as measured by this standardized test. This can be seen when we compare the means between the two language groups both overall and at each proficiency level. These scores represent an average of a *S*'s performance on both the listening comprehension and grammar sections of the English Placement Test.[3]

Table 1. ESL Proficiency Level Placement Scores

Group	*Beginning*		*Intermediate*		*Advanced*		*Overall*	
	n	M	n	M	n	M	n	M
Spanish	16	17.9	21	31.3	14	41.7	51	30.3
Japanese	7	20.3	25	30.8	21	42.5	53	31.2
Overall	23	19.1	46	31.1	35	42.1	104	30.8

All *S*s were then tested by a standardized elicited imitation task. The experimenter orally presented one by one the series of randomized experimental sentences to the *S*, who was then asked to repeat each sentence as presented. The set of complex sentences used in this experimental test are exemplified in 13 to 18. As suggested by the examples of the stimulus sentences below, complex sentences 13 to 16 with subordinate *when* clauses varied systematically in branching direction. That is, they were either right- or left-branching where the subordinate clause was either pre- or postposed to the main clause. Sentences 13 and 14 varied in branching direction right in 13 and left in 14 but did not involve anaphora. Sentences 15 and 16 varied additionally in directionality of the pronominal anaphora in accord with the branching direction differences of each sentence. Right-branching sentences in 15 exemplify foward pronominal anaphoras; sentences in 16 exemplify left-branching with backward pronomimal anaphoras. Comparison of sentences 15 and 16 with sentences 13 and 14 allowed us to test the factor of branching-differences independent of the direction of anaphora.

Stimulus Sentences

No Anaphora

13   *RB* a. The boss informed the owner when the worker entered the office.
                   b. The worker called the owner when the engineer finished the plans.
14   *LB* a. When the actor finished the book, the woman called the professor.
                   b. When the man dropped the television, the woman hugged the child.

Pronominal Anaphoras

15   *RB* a. The man answered the boss when he installed the television.
             b. The worker introduced the foreman when he entered the room.
16   *LB* a. When he delivered the message, the actor questioned the lawyer.
             b. When he prepared the breakfast, the doctor called the professor.

Sentences exemplified in 17 and 18 were also included in the experimental sentence batteries. These sentences involved no overt syntactic embedding or branching-direction differences. Sentence 17 involved two juxtaposed clauses with redundant subjects, and sentence 18 involved juxtaposed clauses with redundant verb phrases. Results of imitation on these sentences provided us with baseline linguistic competences for each of the two language groups by testing *S*s' ability to imitate two-clause structures which did not involve branching direction or anaphora.

Juxtaposed Sentences—Covariate Factor

*S*VO:*S*VO

17   a. *The man* discussed the article; *the man* studied the notebook.
          b. *The student* opened the briefcase; *the student* erased the board.

S*VO*:S*VO*

18   a. The mayor *dropped the letter*; the diplomat *dropped the letter*.
          b. The student *discussed the test*; the professor *discussed the test*.

Sentences varied as to whether subject of VP was redundant. Italicized notation refers to position of redundancy.

By utilizing the results provided by the imitation of these juxtaposed sentences as a covariate in our factorial design, we were able to test whether differences between the two language groups which might result on the experimental sentences 13 to 16, which involved subordination and anaphora, *were* due to these hypothesized factors of embedding and anaphora and were not just due to factors of complex sentence formation in general. We hypothesized that if significant differences are found on the experimental sentences when baseline syntactic competence differences, such as those on these juxtaposed sentences, are removed, then the results would indicate that significant differences between the two language groups were due to the specified experimentally varied structural properties of these sentences, namely, BD and direction of anaphora.

All sentences were equalized in syllable length (15 syllables) and approximately in word length (10 words). In addition, attempts were made to keep sentences pragmatically neutral so that anaphora was not more likely to be pragmatically and astructurally determined in one condition over another. Stereotypical pairings of agents, patients, and actions in the two clauses were avoided.

All *S*s were pretrained on all lexical items used in the stimulus sentences prior to the actual testing. All *S*s, at least 24 hours prior to the experimental testing, were given bilingual lists with all the lexical items used in the stimulus sentences written both in their first language and in English. *S*s were instructed to study these words in English for the experiment. Immediately prior to testing, each *S*'s comprehension of these words was checked in English. Testing did not begin until the *S* achieved 100 percent comprehension of all items in English. There were 18 sentences in total.

RESULTS

Results on amount correct confirm that the PBD typology is a significant predictor of a second language learner's processing and acquisition of these complex structures.[4] Second language learners are sensitive to differences in PBD between the first and second language and use this sensitivity to formulate hypotheses about the second language, specifically hypotheses about anaphora.

Overall, as shown in Table 2, *language group* was significant main factor as measured by an analysis of variance (ANOVA) on amount correct for sentences both with and without anaphora with juxtaposed sentences in 17 and 18 as covariate. Adjusted means due to the extraction of covariate and upon which F tests are based are shown in parentheses. Speakers of Spanish, where the PBD of the first language matched that of English, imitated the English complex structures both with and without anaphora significantly more easily

Table 2.   Analyses of Amount Correct (Score Range 0 to 3)

Overall Means
No anaphora (cf. sentences 13–14)
Language Group: $F(1,97) = 27.32, p = .0000$

Japanese:	.37	(.45)
Spanish:	1.37	(1.26)

Pronominal anaphoras (cf. sentences 15–16)
Language Group: $F(1,97) = 19.58, p = .0000$

Japanese:	.67	(.72)
Spanish:	1.57	(1.45)

Level Means
No anaphora (cf. sentences 13–14)

	Japanese		Spanish		F
Beginning	.00	(.33)	.82	(.86)	N.S.
Intermediate	.18	(.30)	1.57	(1.47)	$(1,43) = 28.53, p = .000$
Advanced	.72	(.71)	1.71	(1.46)	$(1,32) = 6.28, p = .02$

Pronominal anaphoras (cf. sentences 15–16)

	Japanese		Spanish		F
Beginning	.07	(.45)	.56	(.62)	N.S.
Intermediate	.40	(.54)	1.86	(1.74)	$(1,43) = 31.98, p = .000$
Advanced	1.19	(1.18)	2.28	(1.99)	$(1,32) = 6.46, p = .02$

than speakers of Japanese where there is a mismatch in PBD between the first and second languages.

It should be emphasized here again that the two language groups were equivalent in terms of general ESL ability as measured by the standardized ESL test, and that these differences between the groups hold above and beyond those baseline differences which were extracted by our covariate, score on juxtaposed sentences.

As suggested by the means shown in Table 2, Japanese *S*s had a great deal of difficulty with these complex sentence structures. The fact that the groups differed significantly on these sentences both with and without anaphors suggested that BD holds as a main factor independent of directionality of anaphora.

However, second language learners do use this sensitivity to the PBD to constrain their hypotheses about anaphora. It can be seen in Figure 1 that sentences with forward pronominal anaphoras are significantly easier than sentences with backward pronominal anaphoras for Spanish *S*s at the intermediate level. There is no significant difference between sentences with foward and backward pronominal anaphors for the Japanese *S*s at this or any other level.

First language acquisition studies which investigated English-speaking children's acquisition of these complex sentence structures indicated that the effects of directionality are developmental. Results on second language acquisition indicate that before second language learners can begin to generate hypotheses about how complex structural properties of the second language interact, they must first be at a minimal level of competence in the second language. Such a level would correspond roughly to that stage where the onset of syntax is evidenced in the first language acquisition. Thus, at the intermediate level, for Spanish *S*s where the first and second language PBD match, sentences

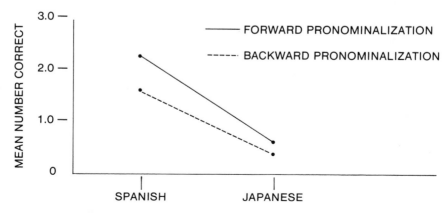

FIGURE 1.   Amount Correct on Forward and Backward Pronominalization Intermediate Level: Direction × Group $F(1,44) = 7.38$, $p = .0094$

with forward pronominal anaphoras are significantly easier than sentences with backward pronominal anaphoras.

Further, at the intermediate level, where the effects of directionality are evident, an analysis of the imitation errors made which involved anaphora also evidenced PBD as a constraint on anaphora. Anaphora errors in this analysis all maintained a two-clause structure but involved some revision of the anaphoric relation. As shown in Table 3, a significant main effect for *language group* was again found when the number of anaphora errors were analyzed. As shown, Japanese *S*s made significantly more anaphora errors than the Spanish *S*s did on these structures which involved anaphora.

In addition, analysis of the errors made by the Spanish and Japanese *S*s at the intermediate level evidenced different types of errors made by each language group. Japanese *S*s in imitating sentences with forward pronominal anaphoras, for example, sentences in 19a and b, were often only able to maintain the first clause without giving any of the right-branching subordinate clauses. This type of error, as shown in Table 4, accounted for 52 percent of the errors made on these right-branching sentence structures for the Japanese. Such first-clause errors accounted for only 11 percent of the errors made on sentences with backward pronominal anaphors for the Japanese *S*s as shown in Table 4. Moreover, as shown in the examples in 19, when Japanese *S*s produced some version of the right-branching structure, they did so in a way that substantially revised or denied the anaphoric relation.[5] That is, in 19a, a *S* simply repeated the first clause, the main clause, without giving any of the right-branching subordinate clauses which contained the pronominal anaphora. In 19b, a *S* similarly repeated the first clause and reduced the right-branching clause which contained the pronominal anaphora to a prepositional phrase.

Table 3. *Anaphora Error* (with Pronominal Anaphors)

Intermediate Level
   Language Group: $F(1,44) = 6.30, p = .0158$
Means
   Japanese: .58
   Spanish: .17
Error Analyses:

Table 4. One-Clause Repetitions (i.e., Repetition of First Clause Only) of Sentences with Pronominal Anaphors (cf. 15–16), Percent of Error

Intermediate Level

Language group	RB (cf. 15)	LB (cf. 16)
Japanese	52	11
Spanish	6	25

On the other hand, as shown in Table 4, for Spanish Ss at the intermediate level, one-clause errors accounted for only 6 percent of the errors made on sentences with forward pronominal anaphors and 25 percent of the errors on sentences with backward pronominal anaphors. In contrast to the types of errors made by the Japanese Ss, Spanish Ss appeared to be often able to make some sense of the anaphora even when they had trouble with the specific anaphoric relation involved. For example, in 20, a Spanish S appeared to have difficulty with the backward direction of the anaphora relation and thus converted the structure to a double pronoun structure.

Examples of Errors

19   *Japanese*
        a. Stimulus: The man introduced the policeman when he delivered the plans.
            Response: The man introduced the policeman . . .
        b. Stimulus: The mayor questioned the president when he entered the room.
            Response: Mayor questioned the president . . . with the diplomat.

20   *Spanish*
        Stimulus: When he prepared the breakfast, the doctor called the professor.
        Response: When he finished the breakfast he called to the professor.

As shown in Table 5, in contrast to the types of errors made by the Japanese Ss, the greatest percentage of errors made by the Spanish Ss were what we characterized as lexical errors. The lexical errors considered here all maintained the two-clause structure and did not involve any revision of the anaphora relation but did involve a substitution of a lexical item not considered a synonym for a lexical item in the stimulus sentence. For example, in 21 a, a S substituted the word *acts* for *plans*. A similar example is shown in 21 b.

Examples of Lexical Errors

21   *Spanish*
        a. Stimulus: The man introduced the actor when delivered the plans.
            Response: The man introduced the actor when he delivered the *acts*.
            TBB.
        b. Stimulus: When he delivered the results, the man questioned the lawyer.
            Response: When he delivered the results, the man questioned the *owner*.

Table 5. Lexical Errors Made in Sentences with Pronominal Anaphors Which Maintained the Two-Clause Structure (cf. 15–16), Percent of Error

Intermediate Level

Language group	RB (cf. 15)	LB (cf. 16)
Japanese	13	12
Spanish	44	47

CONCLUSIONS

In conclusion, both processing and acquisition of complex sentence structures have been found to be predicted to a significant degree by the PBD typology. This finding confirms that the universal principle for first language acquisition also holds in second language acquisition.

Such a result suggests one way in which universals of first and second language acquisition may be related. Second language learners are sensitive to differences in the PBD of the first and second language and use this sensitivity to formulate hypotheses about how other complex structural properties interact, specifically anaphora. This suggests that the principle of BD may be part of the essential component for language and is effective in both first and second language acquisition.

With regard to theories of second language acquisition, such results suggest that analyses in terms of a strict or strong version of a traditional contrastive analysis (CA) theory are inadequate. Such a theory claims that there will be interference of surface structure phenomena from the first language in the second language where features do not match between the first and second language (Lado 1957). Thus, for example, CA would predict significant differences in terms of ease of acquisition between the right- and left-branching structures for the Japanese *S*s. Left-branching structures in English match the PBD (left) of Japanese (CA would predict acquisition to be facilitated here) and the right branching do not match (CA would predict interference here). However, as discussed above, there is not significant difference in acquisition between right- and left-branching structures for the Japanese *S*s. Results indicate instead that for both language groups, acquisition patterns of errors cannot be fully explained in terms of this theory.

Similarly, analyses of second language acquisition in terms of a strict creative constructive theory (CCT) (Dulay and Burt 1974) are also inadequate. Work within this framework stresses similarities between the first and second language acquisition processes and minimizes the role of actual syntactic transfer between the first and second language (Gass 1980). The CCT stresses the revival of the general creative process of language learning (Burt and Dulay 1975, p. 210).[6] We can conclude from this then that acquisition of a common second langauge by two different first language groups should *not* evidence effects of the learners' first language experience. Thus, it would predict that errors and developmental trends would be identical for both the language groups studied here—both should be like L1 acquisition of English. However, as our results evidence, the CCT fails to explain the profound systematic differences found here between the two language groups in terms of development and errors made. Where L1 PBD=L2 PBD, L2 acquisition is like L1 acquisition, otherwise not.

Rather, our results suggest that a theory of second language acquisition must be derived from a theory which integrates how more profound and abstract universal principles of acquisition, one such being that which was investigated here, namely, sensitivity to PBD, interact with a second language learner's experience with his or her first language.

Results of our investigation in general seem to accord with a theory of universal grammar (UG) proposed for the first language acquisition process (Chomsky 1980). Consistent with such a theory of UG, our results suggest that the essential language faculty involved in first language acquisition is also involved in second language acquisition. In addition, findings indicate that the parameters of these UG principles need to be and are revised in second language acquisition where particular parametric values between the first and second language do not match. As already discussed, where no revision is necessary, acquisition and processing are facilitated. Where revision is necessary, processing is disrupted and acquisition is delayed.

NOTES

1. This study represents a preliminary report of a dissertation entitled *A Study of the Effects of Principal Branching Direction in Second Language Acquisition: The Generalization of a Parameter of Universal grammar from First to Second Language Acquisition.* (Flynn 1983, Cornell University). I thank Barbara Lust, Jack Carroll, James Gair, and Wendy Snyder for their helpful and insightful comments and discussions. I also thank Wayne Harbert, Carlos Piera, and John Bowers for their comments made on a preliminary version of this study. Special thanks are also owed to Erik Beukenkanp, Pat Marcus, Ida Wolff, Andrea Feldman, and the Board of Education in Englewood, N.J., for allowing me to work with their students and teachers in their programs. Thanks are also given to Yu-Chin Chien for her invaluable assistance with data analyses and to Toshi Nakajima for his help with the translation of the vocabulary lists.

This paper was supported by a graduate research supplement from the Department of Modern Languages and Linguistics, Cornell University, and is based in part upon work supported by the National Science Foundation under grant BNS-7825115.

2. Notably, not all languages instantiate a perfectly consistent branching direction (perhaps only very few, if any, actually do so perfectly). Moreover, all languages appear to allow manipulations of even a basic branching direction, e.g., by pre- or postposing. Languages, however, appear to often allow a "general" characterization in terms of their branching direction over several recursive devices. The precise designation of a PBD is an empirical issue both theoretically and empirically. In this research, languages are chosen for experimental purposes which are basically consistent in BD (e.g., English, Spanish, and Japanese). (See Lust 1983, for a more detailed discussion of these issues.)

3. All *S*s were initially placed into one of three proficiency levels for each of the two subtests administered. Results for each *S* were then averaged over both tests and *S*s were reassigned to levels based on this overall average. The separate proficiency level placements were then compared for each *S*. Placement results were consistent over all three levelings for each *S*.

For a precise explanation on how proficiency levels were determined based on results used by the English Language Institute, University of Michigan, readers are referred to the larger study of which this is a part (Flynn 1983).

4. Only those sentences which maintained the original two-clause structure did not alter in any way the original anaphoric relationship and did not make any major lexical changes (e.g., substitution of nonsynonymous NPs) were scored as correct.

5. As has been noted by Bowers (personal communication), some of the errors made by the Japanese *S*s might be thought to have been due to Japanese *S*s expectations that anaphora such as in the stimulus sentences required a "null" rather than pronominal anaphora. Results of a comparative study of imitation of sentences with null anaphora will be reported in the completed dissertation of which this study is a part (Flynn 1983).

6. This claim was originally made by Burt and Dulay for children learning a second language. However, the CCT has been extended by others in their work with adult second language learners, e.g., Bailey, Madden, and Krashen 1974.

7 Processing Strategies and Morpheme Acquisition

Bill VanPatten
Michigan State University

The possibility of a natural sequence in the acquisition of certain English morphemes by children of other languages has been posited by Dulay and Burt (1973, 1974). Using the same morphemes, Bailey et al. established what they call an order of difficulty for adults learning English as a second language. Accepted as fact is that these two orders differ from each other in several ways. Also accepted as fact is that these orders differ from the order found by Brown (1973) and de Villiers and de Villiers (1973) for children learning English as a first language. In Table 1 the three orders are reproduced, and readers may compare and contrast on their own. What I would like to point out here is that what is striking is the difference in the acquisition of word final /-s/ which serves to mark plurality, third person present, possession, and contracted copula. These morphemes take on the same phonetic shapes in the same environments

Table 1.

Invariant order for L1Ls[a]		Invariant orders for L2Ls	
		Children:[c]	Adults:[d]
-ing		-s (pl.)	-ing
	"in" "on"[b]	-ing	cont. COP
-s (pl.)		cont. COP	-s (pl.)
past irreg.		cont. AUX	articles
-s (poss.)		articles	cont. AUX
	uncont. COP[b]	irreg. past	irreg. past
articles		-s (3rd pers.)	-s (3rd pers.)
	regular past[b]	-s (poss.)	-s (poss.)
-s (3rd pers.)			
	3rd pers. irreg.[b]		
	uncont. AUX[b]		
cont. COP			
cont. AUX			

[a]Brown (1973).
[b]These items are not included in all the L2L studies.
[c]Dulay and Burt (1973).
[d]Bailey, Madden, and Krashen (1974).

(e.g., voiced if the preceding sound is voiced). Researchers have thus asked themselves why phonologically equivalent morphemes are learned at different stages or present differing problems dependent upon which morphemic function they are serving.

It has always struck me as odd that persons researching these morphemes have not categorized them according to syntactic position, i.e., whether they are N-bound morphemes, V-bound morphemes, or belong to the AUX. It makes no sense to compare the V bound /-ing/ with the N bound /-s/ when speaking of acquisition. Nowhere in the literature on either L1 or L2 learners have I found such things as a past tense morpheme used inside the NP or a N morpheme used inside the VP. Learners seem to be well aware of the syntactic combinatory potential of the morphemes they are exposed to, as well as their "syntactic limits."[1]

BACKGROUND AND RATIONALE

Following this line of reasoning, I have taken another look at the data. In Table 2, it can be seen that when ordered according to syntactic criteria, the Dulay and Burt order matches exactly the Bailey et al. order. That is, inside the NP, N-bound morphemes for both adults and children who are L2Ls have the same order. The same is true for the morphemes bound to a V and to those that belong to the AUX. When compared with the order for L1Ls, the orders are also alike, with the exception of possessive /-s/ and articles. The order for these two items is reversed in relation to the order for L2Ls. However, by going back and looking at the rank order scores for the L1L morphemes as calculated by Brown, the mean distance between rank scores is approximately 3.5 (that is, inside the syntactic categories). But the distance between possesive /-s/ and articles is only .67! (See Table 3.) Thus it might be that these two morphemes are acquired simultaneously or at least that this difference in rank score is not significant.

Table 2.   Invariant Order for L2Ls by Category

N	V	AUX
-s (pl.)	-ing	cont. COP
articles	irreg. past	cont. AUX
-s (poss.)	-s (3rd pers.)	

Table 3.   Invariant Order for L1Ls by Category

N		V		AUX	
-s (pl.)	2.33	-ing	2.33	cont. COP	12.66
-s (poss.)	6.33*	irreg. past	6.00	cont. AUX	14.00
articles	7.00*	-s (3rd pers.)	9.66		

Numbers refer to rank ordering.
*Difference between rank orders is only .67, as opposed to a mean of 3.5.

From this information we have an interesting discovery about the major morpheme studies of normal acquirers to this date: that inside syntactic categories, for those morphemes studied, there is no difference as to order between L1Ls and L2Ls! Whether or not this can be taken to assume that L1 acquisition and L2 acquisition are parallel is a matter for further research which involves looking at intermediate steps.[2] However, if there is no difference between L1 and L2 in the final analysis of the *difficulty* of acquisition of these morphemes or in their relative sequence of appearances during acquisition, then several comments can be made about morpheme studies and the acquisition of morphemes.

If the distinction between acquisition and learning is correct (see Krashen 1978, 1981), and so far this distinction has proved to be a powerful explanatory device in language acquisition studies, then it is quite possible that if we tap acquired language rather than learned language, we might see some similarities in L1 and L2 development. In terms of the language learner, it might also be wise to make the distinction between the acquisition of morphemes and the acquisition of syntax, lexicon, register, style, etc. The reason for this is that the human capacity for short-term memory (STM) may not treat all features of a linguistic system in the same way, particularly during production. If the primary goal of an L2L when forming an utterance is to produce something meaningful and there is a time limit (real or perceived), the strain on STM might be such that it is forced to "reject" the storage of certain learned items while the learner is juggling other items of greater importance in order to speak.[3] It seems to me that syntax (word order, grammatical relations, and the like) would take on a certain higher level of priority for message carrying than would most morphemes. Likewise, lexical item choice would supersede morpheme choice and store if there is strain on STM. When investigating learner speech, researchers need to be aware of just what they are tapping, acquired or learned grammar, and what the interaction is between STM and these two grammars. It appears reasonable that if we take into consideration this interaction, then L1 interference can indeed be found at the syntactic and lexical levels as the L2L might deem these areas more important for conscious control and may attempt to produce "beyond his capability." Morphemes, on the other hand, may be ignored by the learner for the most part and be used just as they exist in the acquired system with little or no conscious control. This does not mean that they cannot be monitored like any other item, only that this is less likely to occur under conditions where the learner ignores form and is interested mostly or solely in the message.

In sum, high-priority items are apt to be subjected to monitoring if the conditions are right while lower-level priority items are not. Thus, morpheme studies may lend themselves more to the kinds of investigation where L1 and L2 similarities are being researched. Syntax and lexical items lend themselves more to research where interference is being investigated. This conclusion, I believe, deserves to be further investigated, for it may lie at the heart of the interference/noninterference controversy.

Returning to such things as "invariant orders" and "accuracy orders" categorization according to syntactic criteria has several important consequences. First, it raises the point of criticisms leveled at acquisition studies similar to those done by Dulay and Burt. The most well-known criticism is from Rosansky (1976). While indeed she is correct that there is individual difference as to rank orders and accuracy orders among groups of learners as well as individual difference in longitudinal development of single learners, all her subjects, with the exception of one, follow the accuracy orders under syntactic categories expounded here. That is, it may be that learners as a whole may vary as to whether they acquire X V-bound morpheme in comparison with Y N-bound morpheme, but this does little, if anything, to alter the order inside the NP itself. Likewise, the acquisition of a N-bound morpheme has little to do with the acquisition of the V-bound morphemes. With all but one of Rosansky's subjects, this seems to be the case.[5]

A second more obvious point raised by the way in which I have organized the data is, "Why are the orders the same?" Why, for example, is /-ing/ easier (or, possibly, acquired first) to be followed by past tense, and subsequently by third person /-s/? It is to this question that the second part of this paper is addressed.

DATA FROM FL STUDENTS

As mentioned earlier, several explanations for the order of morphemes elicited in the studies under consideration here have been attempted. Larsen-Freeman (1976) concluded that the order was dependent upon the naturally occurring frequency of the morphemes in native speaker adult speech. Hatch (1975) also recurred to this explanation but added that other factors may combine with frequency to either reduce its effect or increase it. This sort of approach, however, deviates from an ultimate goal of L2 research: to posit a theory of language learning on a universal level. The explanation of frequency of occurrence places emphasis on the morphemes themselves rather than on the processing strategies utilized by the learner during intake and offers little if any insight to what the learner is doing during the acquisition process. These explanations differ from those offered by researchers such as Slobin (1973) and Ervin-Tripp (1974) in which the learner is seen as possessing operating prinicples which filter input. In this section, I will take the approach that the learner is active[6] during acquisition, and I will attempt to explain the previously examined orders in terms of one language learning principle. In order to do so, however, I will have to look at some data from learners of a language other than English, a recourse which I believe will show its value as the discussion progresses.

A sore point of the research in L2 acquisition to this date is that not much has been done with L2 learners of other languages, at least not in terms of acquisition studies. The bulk of evidence that we have on L2 learning is based on learners of English as an L2 here in this country. We have no evidence that there is a natural order for learners of Spanish, let us say, or German. While important research is surfacing more and more frequently which deals with FL learners, we really have no cross-linguistic evidence to support our claims about acquisition orders, especially when we have no evidence for the explanation of them. The claim of frequency of occurrence as a determinant in order, for example, is seriously cast into doubt when one looks at data of students of Spanish in the United States. A persistent problem for these learners is the acquisition of adjective agreement, specifically the acquisition of word final /-a/. Here we have a case of early exposure to the item, high frequency in the natural language, and emphasis placed on it during overt instruction. Why then does this item produce much lower accuracy scores than something like the morpheme /-aba-/, a Spanish past tense morpheme? (See Dvorak and VanPatten, in progress, for work being done on learners of Spanish.) Why is the copular verb "estar," a high-frequency item in the classroom, not acquired at all or is acquired rather late in the development of the L2?

In 1979, Dvorak and VanPatten began a study of 10 adults learning Spanish as a FL at Rutgers University. The students were followed through the course of an entire year, being taped every two weeks for oral production and also tested for comprehension and grammar in a separate component. While data analysis has yet to be completed, some very interesting phenomena appear in the transcripts of the recording sessions. Often the experimenter (E) would supply the subject (S) with a lexical item or structure in a question or during the conversation, and the S seemed to selectively focus on what was just said. Examine the following interchange:

> E: ¿Cómo están ellos? (How are they?)
> S: Son contentos. (They are happy.)

The correct copula choice in Spanish for the above situation is "estar," that used by the E. But the S ignored the verbal cue in the question and produced an utterance of his own with the verb "ser." No overt monitoring occurred (i.e., there was no self-correction), and he appeared not even to have noticed the discrepancy between what was provided as input and what he himself said.

As an agrument against position of the verb and its possible (lack of) saliency, note the following interchange with the same S which occurred immediately after the above episode:

> E: Y ellos, ¿cómo están? (And them? How are they?)
> S: Son contento también. (They're fine, too.)

In the experimenter's follow-up question, "están" appears in sentence-final position and bears strong stress. Clearly the S was not focusing on the copula at all during intake.

Another example is the following misuse of the definite article by another S:

> E: ¿Y qué hace el hombre? (And what's the man doing?)
> S: La hombre corre. (The man is running.)

"La" is a feminine article in Spanish and does not co-occur with masculine nouns. The S ignored the article in the question and produced something else.

Before discussion of these data, I would like to offer one more interchange which is slightly different. In this interchange, the E was not asking a question but was providing a lexical item for the S, who was groping for something with which to finish his sentence:

> S: . . . y él, uh, él, uh, uh . . . (and he, uh . . .)
> E: Se sentó. (He sat down.)
> S: Sentó, sí. (He sat, yes.)

The S, in confirming the lexical item, did not repeat all that he heard, but only the verb stem and tense affix. The reflexive pronoun "se" was omitted. It is to be noted here that these three interchanges were not atypical in that they occurred with almost all the subjects, both "good learners" and "poorer learners."

Two questions come to mind: why didn't these Ss pick up things that they heard in a question or preceding statement, particularly when the statement length was indeed short and should not have been taxing memory all that much? Why didn't the Ss stop and overtly monitor for these items?

The second question can quickly be answered by recurring to the Monitor Model. Obviously, these Ss' attention was on message and not form. Therefore, the monitor was not activated at these points in the conversations. The first question, however, is a little more intriguing and requires a bit of speculation. For the moment, we need to put ourselves in the learner's place.

When confronted with normally paced speech (or even slower speech directed at a learner), what is it that we are going to attend to? If our goal is to answer the questions with correct information, then content is of utmost importance. If we want to answer the question *and* at the same time learn something about the language we are speaking, then we might also attend to form. In the first case, given the question "¿Cómo están ellos?" if we heard only "cómo" and "ellos" we could answer the question without attending to the copula; particularly if the referent is clear (in this case the S was looking at a picture). The copula we use in the answer comes from our own repertoire of grammar and we may not notice any discrepancies. Since we have placed emphasis on communication only, that is all that preoccupies us.

If we imagine a longer string to be processed for communication, the effects of this "communication strategy" are even more evident. As the learner attempts to process the information and his focus is on content only, "high-powered" semantic items receive priority. Coupled with the effects of STM, upon which a communication strategy must depend, it is not difficult to reason why some items become intake and others do not. "Semantic clout" or "commucative impact" (for lack of better terms) thus orders items in a string as to their relative importance for understanding the message.

VanPatten (1980) offered that most items taught during a first-year course are not acquired, i.e., do not reach the 90 percent accuracy level. Plann (1974) also suggested the same but was referring to an elementary school immersion program where a "classroom dialect" developed from which the learners did not progress toward the FL norm. I would like to suggest here that in natural communication in the classroom, or even during quasi-communicative inter-actions such as picture description and story summarization, students function largely under this communication strategy, thus attending to items which carry more semantic clout than others or are perceived as having more semantic clout than others.

Evidence also comes from Schumann (1978) and Krashen (1978). In developing the link between pidginization and L2 acquisition, Schumann cites the lack of progress of Alberto, who, as is evident from the data in Schumann's study, is using a communication-based strategy in speaking. More than likely he is also using a communication-based strategy during listening. Krashen's "minimal monitor user" also explains why she "ignores the little words while speaking." But the unmentioned counterpart must exist: that she also ignores the little words while listening to another's speech.

If a communication-based strategy is so prevalent among language learners at the adult level (especially in the early stages), then how do they ever progress beyond a "pidginized" state? The answer, I believe, lies in something suggested earlier: that there is a second comprehension strategy available to learners which also involves focus on form. This strategy, however, may only be utilized when automaticity of the communication strategy is achieved, i.e., the elements of the utterance which render its meaning to the L2L have become part of the acquired system and comprehension does not involve some sort of mental juggling between the language equivalencies of L2 and the native language, and the L2L is actually trying to learn something. The learner who no longer needs to invoke equivalencies now has the time and the capacity to "scan" the utterance for new linguistic information and make use of it. As the learner interacts more and more on a communicative level of language use during the course of learning, the learning-based strategy is what *allows* him to progress and ultimately acquire items that he lacked before.

Returning to the problem of overt monitoring, it becomes evident that the comprehension processing strategies outlined here are integrally related to production strategies as well. The Ss in the Dvorak and VanPatten study self-corrected for items they perceived to be of most importance and ignored items they deemed of lesser importance. Moreover, the ignored items during production are generally those that are ignored in the types of interchanges which we examined earlier. As proposed by Krashen, the monitor can be used when focus during production is on form and it principally contains learned grammatical items for use as a "repair." Since the learners examined here all have the relevant rules for COP choice and adjective agreement as evidenced by paper and pencil tests administered as part of the research, one must conclude that the monitor and the comprehension strategies are linked by the same general principle for use: focus on form vs. focus on message, and communication necessarily involves items which yield the highest semantic or referential impact as perceived by the learner. It is interesting to note that so little attention has been paid to comprehension in the literature on FL and L2 learning and that the monitor is thought of in terms of production only. Ironically, the monitor model itself is based upon what happens during comprehension, for the acquisition/learning distinction relies on input and intake. The latter terms describe what is heard (or read) and not what is produced.

If these two processing strategies exist and "semantic clout" of grammatical and lexical items is seen as the key to the communication strategy, our next question is to see if there is a relation between processing and the proposed morpheme orders.

SEMANTIC CLOUT AND MORPHEMES

Recall from the first part of this paper that any discussion of morphemes is most accurate when morphemes are compared with other morphemes of the same syntactic class. Thus, the acquisition of V-bound morphemes should be compared only with the acquisition of other V-bound morphemes. Likewise, the N-bound morphemes should be compared only with other N-bound morphemes. Using this criterion, an accuracy order for V-bound morphemes was established for all learners of English:

> -ing
> irregular past
> -s (3rd per.)

It seems that our conclusion about semantic clout and comprehension strategies holds for these morphemes. In naturally occurring speech directed at learners (i.e., *not* the free-flowing discourse that exists among native adult speakers of English), /-s/ as a third person marker carries the least semantic clout. That is, the person of any verb can be determined by attention to the obligatory subject that precedes it. If the NVN=SVO processing strategy exists for all learners (as has been documented in the literature on L1 Ls and L2 Ls), then attention will be paid to the subject of the verb and the affix /-s/ becomes communicatively unimportant. On the other hand, the affix /-ing/ occurs very seldom with coreferential adverbials in speech directed toward L1 Ls (focus on the "here and now") and toward L2 Ls (picture descriptions such as "What is he doing?" "Where is she going?" and in class action description such as "What is Abdul doing? Is he sleeping?" all of which unequivocably focus in on the here and now). The learner attends to the /-ing/, as it is the only thing in the utterance which gives him temporal reference. Past tense morphemes (regular and irregular) are in the middle area where they usually occur with past tense adverbials, if not in the same utterance at least at the initiation of a discussion and periodically throughout. Frequent is the case in the ESL classroom where the teacher uses such lexical items as "last night" or "this morning" when wishing to use the past tense for conversation. The learner is more likely to pay attention to these items than to the verbal affix in order to establish temporal referents. In their interaction with children, it has been shown that mothers often rely on similar strategies in delivering speech to children, and my guess is that native speakers also use adverbials when addressing early-stage nonnatives to facilitate comprehension.

In general, what we see happening is that learners are paying attention to items in an utterance or conversation which have more semantic clout than their corresponding morphemes simply because these other items are whole lexical items which the learner feels he should process for meaning. Therefore, /-ing/ receives more attention than /-s/, since there is seldom anything else in the utterance that carries the same semantic information, and /-d/ falls somewhere in between, depending upon how often the learner is "forced" to focus on it in order to grasp tense.

The same can be shown to be true of the N-bound morphemes:

-s (pl.)
articles
-s (poss.)

Unless an adverbial of quantity co-occurs with a N, /-s/ carries the semantic value of number and the learner relies on it for marking singularity and plurality.[7] However, articles and /-s/ possessive do little if anything to render the meaning of the utterance to a learner, at least in the early stages. Possession can almost always be inferred from word order and what the learner knows about logical relationships (e.g., "John book," without an intervening verb such as "reads" or "writes," can only mean "John has/owns a book"). This renders the /-s/ possessive morpheme rather unimportant for communication. As for the argument that articles carry the value of definite/indefinite, based on classroom observation and my own experience at ESL teaching, I think that this semantic conception is of minimal importance during the early stages. The speech directed toward learners is often so simplified that such things as defi-nite/indefinite may not play as large a role as something like singular/plural.[8] To demonstrate this, a detailed analysis of learner input speech needs to be completed. Unfortunately, I cannot present that here and though one regrets having to fall on the feeble excuses of "lack of time" or "lack of space" or "beyond the scope of this paper," I must do it here. Nonetheless, it should not detract from the logic of this argument or the data presented thus far. As more data are accumulated on learner input via discourse analysis, I feel the hypotheses and assertions made in this paper will bear themselves out.

CONCLUSIONS

All that we have been saying up to this point can be summarized as follows: Because of the nature of the speech directed toward learners (both L1Ls and L2Ls), reliance upon certain morphemes for semantic information decreases if other lexical items bearing the same information co-occur in the sentence *or* the morpheme is not important to understand the sentence as a whole and respond to it. As this reliance decreases, so do the propensities to process the morpheme and acquire it. Only as learners become more proficient at meaning processing (i.e., grasping the meaning of an utterance becomes automatic) and strain is taken off the working properties of memory and the processing system(s), do they begin to attend to and acquire these less communicatively important morphemes. The consequences of this hypothesis are far-reaching for language acquisition studies and for language teaching. In terms of the latter, it explains why, in a given year of instruction of FL, learners may learn certain morphemes but not acquire them. As the learners advance in the classroom, the length of the utterances directed at them (as well as those that they are expected to produce) becomes greater and greater. This lengthening of the utterance, however, proceeds at a much faster rate than the ability of the learner to process meaning. In other words, he is forced to process beyond his ability. Since he is always groping for meaning, he *seldom* gets out of the communication-based strategy to apply a learning strategy. In our race to expose language learners to the many grammatical and morphological points of the FL or L2 in the first year, we do not allow enough time for certain processing mechanisms to become automatic, and consequently not much other than vocabulary is acquired. What would be most beneficial for acquisition in the classroom is for teachers to keep utterances (during any type of communicative or quasi-communicative practice) at the levels (plural because not all students will be at the same level at the same time) where students can readily process them for meaning, but at the same time be challenging enough so that the student will "scan" with his learning strategy.

In terms of acquisition studies, this hypothesis sets us on a different track than before. Attempts to explain the acquisition of morphemes in purely linguistic terms, as opposed to communicative impact/semantic clout, has led us away from what people are doing with language when acquiring one: communicating (grasping and sending meanings). More research is needed, though, detailing the acquisition of such morphemes in a longitudinal manner. Are there sufficient cases, if any, where a learner acquires /-s/ third person before /-d/ past tense and the rank order difference between the two is significant? Are there cases where a learner acquires communicatively "less important" morphemes before those with more semantic clout? If there are, the hypotheses presented here will have to be reevaluated or discarded. But if not, the acquisition of morphological and grammatical structures may need to be examined in light of their role in communication and how learners process them during communicative interaction.

NOTES

1. Since the original writing of this paper, the work done by Andersen (1978) has come to my attention. He too worked with morphemes in terms of NP, VP and AUX. The difference between his work and mine lies in the explanations that we offer for the order and acquisition of morphemes. Furthermore, I included L1 acquisition as part of the universal order and explanation of such order.

2. I do not advocate here that the *steps* in arriving at 90 percent accuracy of any morpheme are necessarily the same for L1Ls and L2Ls simply because the sequences of acquisition or the order of difficulty is the same. Wode (1978) and Heubner (1979) argue convincingly against such a conclusion. In any event, two identical products do not necessarily imply that two identical processes were at work to bring them about.

3. There also exists the problem of long-term memory (LTM). One may ask if certain items are even *accessed* from LTM for utterance production if the conditions of time and focus on message are present. We are dealing with rather (normally) high-speed processes during recall, and if there is a time constraint and focus away from form, then the role of LTM must also be called into question.

4. Tarone (this volume) has recently argued that variability in interlanguage may be viewed in Labovian terms, i.e., as a result of the degree of attention paid to speech. This, however, does not necessarily negate the distinction between unconscious internalized rules and forms.

5. The one Rosansky subject which did not fit into a syntactically categorized analysis of morphemes was the one who seemed to have already acquired almost all of the morphemes, and his scores were generally above the 90 percent mark anyway.

6. In using the term "active," I do not wish to give the reader the idea that I see the learner consciously employing strategies. At best, it can be said of all operating principles and strategies that often they are not thought about and sometimes they are purposefully used.

7. In an interesting study of the deletion/aspiration of final /s/ in Caribbean Spanish, Terrell (1978) points out that in the NP, *something* must be present (usually in the first modifier of the head N) to mark plurality. Thus, at least in dialects of Spanish, the overt marking of plurality somewhere in the NP has to occur even in the speech of those who have a high propensity to elide or aspirate final /s/, which, like English, serves to mark plurality in Spanish. It would be interesting to see if this "requirement" is a universal phenomenon in languages where there is plurality marking and adjective concordance.

8. Pidgins are an interesting case of what might be viewed as "morpheme acquisition in reverse." That is, these hybrids are well known for the absence of such things as articles rather than their "obligatory presence." Usually, however, they do mark plurality. This, I feel, is further evidence for the primacy of plural markers over articles for communicative purposes. Pidgins are known to be languages which arise out of the simple need to communicate.

B. L2 Universals

8 Accounting for Adult Acquisition of Relative Clauses: Universal Grammar, L1, and Structuring the Intake

Christian Adjémian and Juana Liceras
University of Ottawa

In developing a theory of the acquisition of nonnative grammatical knowledge, we must bear in mind that at least three major factors may greatly influence the form and properties of the learner's emerging nonnative grammar. These are:

- Universal grammar: the set of biologically specified parameters that define the notion "possible human language."
- Attained linguistic knowledge: the grammatical knowledge of the native language and of any other language(s) familiar to the learner.
- Metalinguistic abilities: the learner's capacities to reflect on language and to perceive (perhaps surface) regularities in incoming linguistic data.

These three major cognitive capacities will interact, in ways we still do not understand, to shape the learner's hypotheses about the target language grammar. In this paper we will examine how the interaction of these three major forces may shape the learner grammar in the acquisition of a set of properties of restrictive relative clauses by adult learners of nonnative languages.[1]

Second language research on relative clauses to date has focused on functional and distributional problems (e.g., Ioup and Kruse 1977, Gass 1979). In this paper we examine the internal structure of restrictive relative clauses in three languages and the problems the grammars of these structures pose to nonnative learners. We begin with a brief discussion of the relevant properties of the grammar of restrictive relatives in the three target languages we are concerned with: English, French, and Spanish. We then outline one generally accepted proposal for modeling these properties, and then discuss its implications for acquisition theory. This is followed by a presentation of our experimental framework, our data, and our conclusions.

RESTRICTIVE RELATIVES IN ENGLISH, FRENCH, AND SPANISH

The major properties of restrictive relative clauses in these three languages can be summarized as follows:[2]

- All undergo *wh*-movement, a rule which moves a relative pronoun from its base-generated position into an empty slot in the COMP node, yielding an intermediate structure, as in 1, which has the phrase structure given in Figure 1.

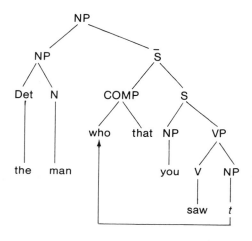

FIGURE 1. Result of wh-movement

Relevant examples of the same intermediate step in French and Spanish are in 2: ± = trace of the moved constituent.

1   a. The man [[/ /that] you saw who]
    b The man [[/who/ that] you saw *t*]

2   a. L'homme [[/ /que] tu as parlé auquel]
    b. L'homme [[/auquel/ que] tu as parlé *t*]
    c. El hombre [[/ /que] tú has hablado a quien]
    d. El hombre [[/a quien/que] tú has hablado *t*]
    "The man to whom you spoke."

- All three languages permit only a single element in COMP in surface structure.

3   a. *The man to whom that you spoke.
    b. *L'homme auquel tu as parlé.
    c. *El hombre a quien que tú has hablado.

All three languages have a rule deleting elements in the COMP node. Compare the sentences in 4, corresponding to the structures in 1 and 2.

4   a. The man [[who Ø] you saw *t*]
       b. L'homme[[auquel Ø tu as parlé *t*]
       c. El hombre [[a quien Ø] tú has hablado *t*]

- All three languages permit prepositional phrases in COMP. This is shown in 4 for Spanish and French, and in 5 for English.

5   the man [[to whom] you spoke *t*]

- All three languages permit the complementizer, i.e., the morphemes *that*, *que*, *que*, to appear in COMP by deletion of the relative pronoun.

6   a. The man that you saw.
       b. L'homme que tu as vu.
       c. El hombre que tú has visto.

Our three target languages show some interesting differences in the structure of their relative clauses.

- English allows the optional deletion of any or all elements in COMP except in the case of relativization of the subject.[3] See the following examples:

7   a. The man who you saw.
       b. The man that you saw.
       c. The man you saw.
       d. The man who saw you.
       e. The man that saw you.
       f. *the man saw you.

- French and Spanish do not permit empty COMPs and require deletion of noun phrase relative pronouns in COMP:

8   a. *el hombre quien/el cual/Ø tú has visto . . .
       b. *l'homme qui/lequel/Ø tu as vu . . .

- French in addition requires the complementizer *que* to take the form *qui* in the case of relativization of the subject. Compare 9b with 9c, in contrast to the Spanish (9a).

9   a. El hombre que ha llegado . . .
       b. *L'homme que est arrivé . . .
       c. L'homme qui est arrivé . . .

The rule that performs this operation is schematically given in 10. We shall call it the *que/qui* rule.[4]

- English allows preposition stranding while French and Spanish do not.[5]

10   a. The man that/who you spoke to.
       b. *El hombre que has hablado con.
       c. *L'homme que tu as parlé à.

RESTRICTIONS ON COMP AND ACQUISITION

Some of the differences seen earlier are fairly subtle, yet they must be acquired by adults learning these languages. Examining such subtle phenomena, we feel, will allow us better to test the power of our hypotheses about acquisition. This is our major motivation in utilizing the rigor of a formalized framework in second language acquisition research. Without such a framework the details of the internal structure of the relative clauses would not be clearly understood, and therefore researchers would miss the major acquisition problems posed by the grammars of these structures. A formal analysis forces us to consider the intricate interaction of rules and conditions on their application as well as properties of specific lexical items. When the structure of the system being acquired is more clearly perceived, hypotheses about acquisition become attainable.

Most of the differences between French, English, and Spanish relative clauses discussed in the preceding section can be accounted for by formulating restrictions on which elements can appear in the COMP node in surface structure. In what follows, we shall sketch an analysis first proposed by Baker (1979a) which provides a reasonable framework for expressing such restrictions and which has some interesting implications for acquisition theory.

Chomsky and Lasnik (1977) propose to modify grammatical theory by eliminating rule ordering and the obligatory application of rules. Instead, rules apply freely and overgeneration by the grammar is constrained by a set of filters, some of which are universal. These apply to the surface structures, marking specific structural configurations as ungrammatical. Thus, for example, in the case of all three languages with which we are concerned a doubly filled COMP node is not permitted in the surface structure of relative clauses (see examples 3a, b, c). This generalization is expressed by a doubly filled COMP filter:

*[a b] (where "a" and "b" are any phrase nodes or the complementizer).

This filter says: in surface structure mark ungrammatical any string with a COMP node containing two phrase nodes.[6]

Baker (1979a) assumes the main lines of the Chomsky and Lasnik analysis. However, he proposes a set of language-specific "permitting filters" rather than the negative output filters of Chomsky and Lasnik. These permitting filters are templates specifying the permissible sequence of elements in the COMP node in surface structure. In other words, they can be read as positive instructions: do not mark as ungrammatical a COMP node containing this configuration in surface structure. The system of positive filters needed in the adult native grammar of English, French, and Spanish can be seen in Figure 2.[7]

Baker (1979a) argues that such language-specific filters are acquired on the basis of direct positive evidence heard by the child. The mere evidencing in a speech sample heard by the learner of a specific configuration suffices to allow the positing of the appropriate permitting filter. That is, hearing NPs in COMP

English	French	Spanish
[e]		
[NP]		
[PP]	[PP]	[PP]
[that]	[que]	[que]
	[qui]	

FIGURE 2. NL Permitting Filters

in restrictive relatives, the child acquiring English will posit an [NP] permitting filter, hearing *that* in the same position, he will acquire a [*that*] permitting filter, and so on. We have elected to develop our discussion in Baker's framework rather than in Chomsky and Lasnik's since specific corrections of putative ungrammatical utterances (negative evidence from the speech community) are not necessary in Baker's theory to lead the learner to the proper analysis. The mastery of Chomsky and Lasnik's negative filters, on the other hand, requires that negative evidence be given to the learner. That is, a child would need specific corrections from the speech community in order to acquire certain of their filters, e.g., the doubly filled COMP filter. Thus these two grammatical models differ in their implications for acquisition theory.

In addition to language-specific filters, both Baker's and Chomsky and Lasnik's analyses suppose that a set of universal filters may exist. Since these are specified by universal grammar, they pose no problem for acquisition. Further detailed discussion of universal and language-specific features and of the issue of positive versus negative evidence and their relevance for linguistic theory and acquisition theory is given in Baker (1979b) and White (1980).

Second Language Acquisition and Filters

In this framework the acquisition of a target language with a set of filters different from those of the native language can theoretically occur in one of two ways, which, following the tradition in second language acquisition research, we shall label as follows:

- (A) *The construction hypothesis*: construct a set of filters pertaining to COMP in restrictive relative clauses as motivated by the primary data.
- (B) *The transfer hypothesis*: assume that the set of filters of L1 are valid in L2 unless proved otherwise by the data.

We feel that a more realistic position implies both hypotheses and that the process of acquisition will involve transfer, construction, and reconstruction as new data are assimilated by the learner. Initial hypotheses may be abandoned or modified by learners as their grammar develops. One interesting possibility discussed by Liceras (1981, 1983) concerns the interaction of properties of universal grammar with these two hypotheses. Assuming a theory of markedness integrated in universal grammar as in Chomsky (1981c), it might be possible, for example, to rank filters on the scale of markedness, thereby developing a hierarchy of filters. If this is the case, it is possible that the least marked filters in the learner's native language are transferred (and perhaps fossilized) and the more marked are abandoned. Such a mixed position, if justified, would indicate that universal grammar plays an important role even in the acquisition of language-specific properties.

In our study, then, we set out to discover how learners of our target languages perceived differences in the distribution of elements in COMP. On the basis of their learner's grammar at one point in time, we attempt to reconstruct what the main lines of the acquisition process must have been in order to project this grammar. Consequently, we looked at evidence of both the transfer and construction of a set of filters. We also looked for evidence of the effects of universal grammar in the acquisition of these target language properties.

THE STUDY

The experiments and results reported here are from a pilot study we carried out in late 1981/early 1982 to develop and test a methodology implied by the framework we adopted. This work has led to further refinements, and we report in work in progress on the acquisition of related structures involving extraction of constituents from embedded sentences (Adjémian and Liceras, in progress). Since the study reported here is a pilot probe, there are areas where the data are not as copious as we would have wished. These are indicated in the text. The fact that our data are limited does prevent making statistical generalizations about the groups that we have studied. But we are quite convinced that our data do clearly suggest how nonnative grammars may be projected and that the framework we adopt leads us to research questions that can push forward acquisition theory and our knowledge of the properties of nonnative grammars (Adjémian 1982).

Subjects

We studied the acquisition of restrictive relative clauses in adult learners at the University of Ottawa (a French/English bilingual university) in first-level language courses.[8] At the time of testing, none of our subjects had been formally taught the properties of restrictive relatives in the target language. They might, however, have been taught properties of relative structures in another previously studied nonnative language. Our subjects were either native speakers of English (Anglophones) learning French or Spanish as a second language, or native speakers of French (Francophones) learning English or Spanish as a second language. We had a total of forty subjects, but unfortunately our testing situation did not allow us to test all these subjects with each of the five tests we used.

Consequently, our tested population varies from test to test, and to make this clear, our tables show absolute frequencies as well as percentage figures. In addition, the groups were not evenly divided among target languages, as the reader will note from our charts.

Tests

We used two oral elicitation tasks: elicited imitation (repetition) and oral translation into the native language. The latter was used to control for comprehension in the repetition test.

We used three written tasks: (1) Grammaticality judgments were elicited by a test that contained sentences to be corrected if judged to be "incorrect." (2) All the sentences in the grammaticality judgment test were then to be translated in written form into the native language, again as a control for comprehension. (3) Finally, we had a set of sentences in the student's native language to be translated in writing into the target language. Sample sentences are given in the Appendix.

Results

Noun Phrase in COMP. There are two issues concerning the appearance of noun phrases in the COMP node that interested us. As can be seen from Figure 2, within the framwork we have adopted, the acquisition tasks involved can be characterized as follows. In order to attain native proficiency Anglophones must not transfer their [NP] permitting filter to either French or Spanish, while Francophones, on the other hand, must acquire an [NP] permitting filter in their grammar of English, and not in their grammar of Spanish. In Tables 1 and 2 we summarize the results we obtained for NPs in COMP. Table 1 gives the results for the oral tasks, Table 2 the results for the written tasks.

Both Francophones and Anglophones repeated NPs in COMP very readily in both target languages on the oral repetition task. We feel that there may be several reasons for this. In the case of Francophones learning English, their willingness to repeat NPs in COMP may indicate that they have already developed an [NP] permitting filter. This would seem to be corroborated by their performance on the two written tasks: grammaticality judgment (87.5 percent) and translation into target language (85 percent) where they readily accepted and produced NPs in COMP. This hypothesis is further supported when we compare these figures with the results obtained on these two written tasks by Francophones learning Spanish (18.75 and 0.0 percent). It seems quite clear from these figures that in their Spanish learner grammars there is no considerable use of an NP permitting filter. Given the hypothesis that permitting filters are acquired on the basis of positive evidence, this is just what we would expect. We feel that the few instances of NP in COMP accepted and produced in Spanish by these subjects on the written tasks may be explained in part by their interpreting the restrictive relatives in our materials as appositives. In both

Table 1.   NP in COMP

	Repetition (%)		Oral translation (%)	
F/E				
NP	75	(12)	50	(8)
que			12.5	(2)
other	12.5	(2)	25	(4)
NR	12.5	(2)	12.5	(2)
F/S				
NP	75	(9)		
que	8.3	(1)	41.7	(5)
qui			41.7	(5)
other	16.7	(2)		
NR			16.6	(2)
A/S				
NP	50	(7)	57.1	(8)
que	14.3	(2)		
that			28.6	(4)
other	28.6	(4)		
NR	7.1	(1)	14.3	(2)
A/F				
NP	33.3	(5)	20	(3)
que	26.7	(4)		
qui	20	(3)		
that			60	(9)
other	6.7	(1)	6.7	(1)
NR	13.3	(2)	13.3	(2)

Spanish and French appositive relatives do permit NPs in COMP. A second explanation is that the Spanish relative pronoun *quien* is being analyzed as *qui*, the French complementizer that does appear in the COMP of restrictive relatives. We found that *quien* is the only relative NP appearing in the Francophones' translation into Spanish.

Much harder to explain, however, is the performance of the Francophones on the Spanish repetition task. Note that they repeated more NPs in COMP in Spanish than did the Anglophones. We propose that two factors may shed some light on this. First, several of our stimuli sentences may not have been long enough to usefully tap the learner's grammatical competence. Second, the similarity in Spanish *quien* and French *qui* noted above led some subjects astray. One subject even repeated a French *qui* for a Spanish stimulus *quien* tallied under "other" in our table) and even with *la cual,* a relative NP as stimulus; another subject produced a quien in oral repetition. Hence, our Francophone subjects may here be influenced by their native language, which is structuring their intake of data from the target language.

Another surprising aspect of our data concerns the occurrence of NP in COMP in oral translation into French by Francophone learners of English (Table 1). The only explanation we see for the high occurrence of NP in COMP in this task (recall that these are ungrammatical in French) is that the learners are influenced by the [NP] permitting filters of their English learner grammar

Table 2. NPs in COMP

	Gr. judgments (%)		Wr. translation (%)		Wr. translation/TL (%)	
F/E						
NP	87.5	(7)			85	(17)
that	12.5	(1)			10	(2)
que			65	(13)		
other			35	(7)	5	(1)
F/S						
NP	18.75	(3)	6.25	(1)	0.0	(0)
que	75	(12)	62.5	(10)	81.25	(13)
quien	6.25	(1)			18.75	(3)
other			31.25	(5)		
(NP + quien)	25	(4)				
A/S						
NP	11.11	(2)	38.89	(7)		
that			55.56	(10)		
que	61.11	(11)			50	(9)
quien	22.22	(4)			44.44	(8)
other			5.55	(1)	5.56	(1)
NR	5.56	(1)				
(NP + quien)	33.3	(6)				
A/F						
NP	6.25	(1)	31.25	(5)		
that			25	(4)		
que	62.5	(10)			20	(2)
qui	18.75	(3)			40	(4)
empty COMP			43.75	(7)		
other	12.5	(2)			40	(4)

under the artificial and pressured conditions of the oral experimental task. This is corroborated by the fact that Francophones produced no NPs in COMP in oral translation into French with Spanish stimuli materials. Note that in written translation into native language (middle column, Table 2) the Francophone group learning English produced no NPs in COMP, and only one was produced by the Francophone learners of Spanish. However, other strategies are used even here, leading to the reasonably large "other" figure. These include avoiding a relative clause entirely, using an appositive in place of a restrictive relative, and sometimes using a verb which changes the structural configuration from that of the stimulus string and requires an oblique (prepositional) relative item. For example, our stimulus *That is the professor whom we need here* was often translated (properly) as *C'est le professeur dont nous avons besoin* with the oblique *dont* (a diachronic fusion of the preposition *de* plus a relative NP). This specific problem can be avoided by more careful choice of stimuli materials. But the general problem indicates the difficulties faced by these early level learners in abstracting out of the complex interaction of the lexical properties of verbs, and the general structural conditions defined by sentence structure, the basic data that will allow them to project a hypothesis about the structure of the restrictive relatives.

Anglophone subjects learning French and learning Spanish repeated NPs in COMP quite readily. We could propose that these subjects are transferring their native language [NP] permitting filter, but in the face of the results for Francophone subjects this hypothesis is not very convincing. Again, it may be that the stimuli materials we used were simply not appropriate to tap their competence. The performance of the Anglophones on the written tasks, however, led to some interesting speculations. Consider the results for Spanish as the target language. Of the instances of NPs in COMP accepted and produced on the grammaticality judgment and written translation into target language tasks, 12 of the total of 14 NPs were instances of the lexical item *quien*. Because of this, we feel that these learners are not generally permitting NPs in COMP but are selectively permitting this single lexical item in this position. We saw the same thing happening with Francophones learning Spanish, as noted above. The reasons for this are two. First, *quien* functions in Spanish much like English *who*, as both an interrogative and a relative pronoun. Second, our Anglophone learners of Spanish are all familiar to some degree with French and may be seeing superficial apparant parallels between *quien* and French *qui*. Note that the Anglophone learners of French do not produce or accept NPs in COMP in French (only one was accepted in the grammaticality judgment task). This may be due to their greater exposure, formally and informally, to French. But they do readily use *qui* in French. This supports our contention that the use of *quien* by Anglophone learners of Spanish may be influenced by their knowledge of French.

It is useful at this point to discuss the implications of this first set of data on the predictions of the permitting filter framework we have adopted. We saw that Francophones were developing an [NP] permitting filter in English but not in Spanish, just as we would expect given the nature of the input data available to them. Yet we also noted that in some cases the learners seem not to be considering a notion as abstract as "NP" but rather restrict their attention to single lexical items (*qui* or *quien*). This supports the framework we have adopted if we consider the global acquisition problem faced by the learner. Permitting filters will be acquired on the basis of direct positive evidence, but this evidence is in the form of utterances or written strings made up of individual lexical items. The learner's first task in the acquisition of syntax is to figure out what abstract grammatical properties these items must have. Thus *qui* or *quien* will be seen not simply as NPs but as very particular items with complex properties. For example, *quien* only permits human antecedents as a relative pronoun and may only have a human referent as an interrogative pronoun (as in English *who*). French *qui* is also restricted to human referents as an interrogative pronoun and as a realtive pronoun. However, *qui* as a complementizer (recall the *que* → *qui* rule above) does not have such a restriction, for being a complementizer, it has no antecedent. The learner's first task, therefore, is to sort out the complex properties of this small but important class of lexical items. We propose that the native language of Francophones might help structure the intake by leading the learner to treat *quien* as *qui* initially. In the case of the Anglophone we suggested that their knowledge of French might be relevant.[9]

Prepositional Phrases in COMP. The acceptability of PPs in COMP should pose no problems for either Anglophones or Francophones in any of our three target languages. Our figures (Table 3) show this to be the case.[10]

In this table, we tabulated separately cases where the stimuli materials contained full relative PPs in the COMP node and those where the relative NP was in the COMP node while the preposition was left behind to the right of the verb, so-called preposition-stranding cases. We can see interesting differences in the acceptability of the stranded versus nonstranded prepositional complements. Considering the differences among the three target languages with respect to preposition stranding, this is not surprising. Recall that English permits stranding while Spanish does not and colloquial French permits stranding in very few instances, such as the Canadian French *la fille que je sors avec = The girl that I go out with*. Using the prepositions *with, con, avec* in our written tasks, the instances of preposition stranding in our data are few. Consider that Anglophones corrected 75 percent of preposition-stranding cases in the French grammaticality judgment task, and either corrected 37.5 percent or avoided (shown as "other") 37.5 percent for a total of 75 percent in Spanish L2. These figures would indicate that Anglophones realize that preposition stranding is a marked property of English,[11] and they are reluctant to attribute

Table 3.   PP in COMP

	Grammaticality judgments (%)				Translation (%)			
	PP in COMP		P Std.		PP in COMP		P Std.	
F/E								
PP	87.5	(7)	12.5	(1)	90	(9)		
Std.		(0)	37.5	(3)		(0)		
Oth.	12.5	(1)	50	(4)	10	(1)		
NR		(0)		(0)		(0)		
F/S								
PP	100	(8)	40	(6)	75	(6)		
Std.		(0)	26.66	(4)	12.5	(1)		
Oth.		(0)	33.34	(5)	12.5	(1)		
NR		(0)		(0)		(0)		
A/S								
PP	88.88	(8)	37.5	(6)	70	(7)	33	(3)
Std.		(0)	25	(4)		(0)	22	(2)
Oth.		(0)	37.5	(6)	20	(2)		
NR		(1)		(0)	10	(1)	45	(4)
A/F								
PP	87.5	(14)	75	(12)	80	(4)	80	(4)
Std.		(0)	25	(4)	20	(1)	20	(1)
Oth.	12.5	(2)		(0)		(0)		(0)
NR		(0)		(0)		(0)		(0)

this property to a target language. This corroborates the conclusion arrived at by Liceras (1981) with a different sample population.

The same remarks can be made concerning Francophones and preposition stranding. Although some stranding is possible in their native language, they are very reluctant to strand in a language they are acquiring, even with the semantic equivalent to a preposition which is amenable to stranding in their NL. In the written translation into target language task, Francophones did not strand at all in the data they produced with English as a target language, and produced only one stranding in Spanish. Interestingly, this single stranding was due to the preposition *avec* in the stimuli materials. We need to test whether such a phenomenon would occur with prepositions like *de*, for example, which cannot be stranded in French. This would help us determine whether learners such as the one that produced this example are treating Spanish like English, a stranding language, rather than like French. Since our Francophone subjects all had some knowledge of English, this a distinct possibility.

Anglophones, even when faced with English stimuli sentences with stranded prepositions, stranded only twice in Spanish and once in French. Interestingly, the subject who produced the preposition stranding in French L2 when presented with a preposition-stranding stimulus sentence also spontaneously produced a stranding in French L2 when presented with a stimulus sentence containing the preposition in the COMP. Once again, it seems to us that the marked character of English as a stranding language is perceived by these learners. This is a clear example of the influence of universal grammar on the acquisition of a nonnative language. Further research on other universal grammar specified properties is clearly a fruitful direction to pursue.

Doubly filled COMP. We hypothesized that doubly filled COMPs, like PPs in COMP, should not be problematic for our subjects. Just as PPs in COMP were easily accepted by our subjects, since all three languages have a [PP] permitting filter, so doulby filled COMPs should generally be rejected in L2, since none of our three languages normally permit doubly filled COMPs. We say normally, since colloquial Canadian French does permit doubly filled COMPs in some restrictive contexts, for example, in restrictive relatives like 11a or in embedded direct questions like 11b.

11   a. l'homme à qui que tu parlais
         the man to whom that you were speaking
       b. Je me demande à qui que tu parlais.
         I wonder to whom that you were speaking.

Spanish appears to have doubly filled COMPS in embedded direct questions 12 but not in restricted relatives.

12   Maria pregunta que quién viene?
      Mary asks that who came?

The Spanish equivalents of sentences 11a and 11b are ungrammatical.

Our subjects did not spontaneously produce doubly filled COMPs on the written translation into TL task. Consequently, only the figures for the repetition and grammaticality judgment tasks are relevant to this aspect of our study. Table 4 displays the results on these two tasks. The figures in parentheses represent the number of doubly filled COMPs accepted or repeated over the total number of doubly filled COMPs in the stimuli materials. In the judgment tasks the only stimuli examples given were interrogatives, while in the repetition task both relatives and interrogatives were given. We decided to extend our study to the COMPs of embedded interrogatives because of the behavior of Spanish, noted above.

In general, subjects were more prone to repeat doubly filled COMPs than they were to judge them acceptable. Once again, our stimuli materials in the repetition task may be partly at fault here. However, we note that in the repetition task subjects did make a distinction between doubly filled COMPs in relatives and those in interrogatives, more easily repeating the latter in the case of Spanish as a target language and in the case of French as a target language. Francophones learning English, however, repeated both types about equally. Since we saw that Spanish has an apparent doubly filled COMP permitting filter for embedded direct questions, it is seductive to think that somehow our learners, both Francophones and Anglophones, are acquiring it. This still leaves the question of why it is that Anglophones should treat French similarly. Since other analyses of these doubly filled COMP configurations are possible, we prefer to leave this question open at the present time.

The data from the grammaticality judgment tasks show that Francophones accepted doubly filled COMPs in English much more readily than did Anglophones in French. This is precisely what the transfer hypothesis would

Table 4.   Doubly Filled COMP

	Repetition (%)		Judgments (%)	
F/E				
Interg.	43.75	(7/16)	50	(4/8)
Relat.	41.66	(10/24)		
Total	42.5	(17/40)		
F/S				
Interg.	83.33	(15/18)	18.75	(3/16)
Relat.	21.42	(3/14)		
Total	56.25	(18/32)		
A/S				
Interg.	76.19	(16/21)	11.11	(2/18)
Relat.	21.42	(3/14)		
Total	54.28	(19/35)		
A/F				
Interg.	60	(3/ 5)	0.0	(0/16)
Relat.	20	(1/ 5)		
Total	40	(4/10)		

predict, since our Francophones did speak the dialect that accepts sentences like 11. Anglophones corrected all instances of doubly filled COMPs in French target language material and all but 11 percent in Spanish target language material, again, as the transfer hypothesis would predict. Yet Francophones accepted 50 percent of English stimuli doubly filled COMPs, although only a small percentage of Spanish stimuli material doubly filled COMPs were accepted. One reasonable hypothesis to explain this difference is to assume that Francophones are more tolerant of elements in COMP in English, since this language shows greater flexibility than French in the distribution of elements in COMP. Further research will have to take into consideration the semantic differences between the two types of sentences we have studied as well as a more careful control utilizing speakers of French who do not readily accept sentences like 11 and utilizing native speakers of Spanish learning French and English.

Empty COMP in relatives. As we saw earlier, English permits empty COMPs in most restrictive relatives while neither French nor Spanish does. We wanted to see if this difference among these three languages would pose a problem for acquisition. The relevant results are displayed in Table 5, where data are organized by the labels E (Empty COMP), NE (Nonempty COMP), or NR (No Response). Comparing Anglophones learning French with Francophones learning English on the repetition task, we can see that Francophones repeated empty COMPs with English as a target language more readily than did Anglophones with French as a target language (65.5 versus 40 percent). In grammaticality judgments, Francophones accepted 75 percent of the empty COMPs in English target language materials while the Anglophones accepted none in French target language materials.[12] In written translation into target

Table 5.   Empty COMP in Restrictive Relatives

	Repetition (%)		Gr. judgments (%)		Wr. translation/TL (%)	
F/E						
E	65.5	(21)	75	(6)	41	(9)
NE	6.4	(2)	25	(2)	59	(13)
NR	28.1	(9)	0	(0)	0	(0)
F/S						
E	83.4	(20)	33.3	(5)	0	(0)
NE	8.3	(2)	66.7	(12)	100	(6)
NR	8.3	(2)	0	(0)	0	(0)
A/S						
E	53.6	(15)	33.3	(6)	18.75	(3)
NE	39.3	(11)	66.7	(12)	81.25	(13)
NR	7.1	(2)	0	(0)	0	(0)
A/F						
E	40	(6)	0	(0)	20	(3)
NE	40	(6)	100	(8)	80	(12)
NR	20	(3)	0	(0)	0	(0)

language, Anglophones produced approximately the same proportion of empty COMPs, regardless of whether the target language was Spanish or French (18.75 percent Spanish and 20 percent French). Francophones, however, produced 41% empty COMPs in their written translations into English but produced no empty COMPs at all in their written translations into Spanish. These figures might lead one to conclude that Anglophones are transferring their empty COMP permitting filter and that they are only beginning to understand that French and Spanish have no such filter. Francophones, on the other hand, have figured out that English has this filter, and are therefore deleting more freely.

However, when we compare these data with the rest of the data for Spanish L2, the picture that emerges is different. If transfer were the main factor in the development of the nonnative grammar, we would expect Anglophones to produce about the same amount of empty COMPs in Spanish as in French, and we would expect Francophones to produce or accept no empty COMPs in Spanish. But we can see that with Spanish as a target language Anglophones accept empty COMPs in repetition less readily than Francophones (53.6 vs. 83.4 percent). Nor do Anglophones judge empty COMPs in Spanish to be acceptable any more easily than do Francophones. In written translation into target language, Anglophones produced empty COMPs while Francophones did not (3 versus 0). However, this represents only 16 percent of the relevant output of these Anglophone learners.[13] We see then that the data would appear to require more than transfer as an explanation. Why do Francophones produce or accept empty COMPs in Spanish at all? Why do they produce or accept empty COMPs in Spanish more readily than do Anglophones in repetition, and at about the same level as Anglophones in judgments, yet they do not produce them at all in written translation?

Several possibilities come to mind. First, we might be dealing with students with very different levels of ability. This, however, is unlikely since for each target language all the students were in the same class and all classes were at the same level. A second possibility is that we do not have enough data to reflect what the learners are doing with respect to these phenomena. Although the total instances of the relevant phenomenon in each test are not very large, they are sufficient for our purposes, we feel, when the results of all tests are compared.

A third possibility is that the prior knowledge of English that the Francophones had influenced their Spanish learner grammars. But this is unlikely in the present case, since we would then expect no discrepancy between oral repetition and judgments on the one hand and written translation into target language on the other.

A fourth, and to us a more interesting and most likely, possibility may be that a performance factor, sentence processing, is interacting with the learner grammar to produce the effects we have observed. Let us assume that Anglophones are becoming aware of the fact that Spanish has no empty COMP permitting filter, just like French. One factor that distinguishes Francophone learners of Spanish from Anglophone learners of Spanish is that the former are being exposed to a language that is quite similar to their own in basic structure. As a consequence, the processing and parsing mechanisms they have developed for their native language can be applied fairly straightforwardly to the TL in a great number of cases. Anglophones, on the other hand, will have more difficulty parsing the spoken TL. Francophones then might simply have been better able to repeat verbatim the stimuli material heard on the oral tasks, therefore producing more empty COMPs on the repetition task than Anglophones. This assumes, of course, that our oral stimuli materials were not of sufficient length to tap directly the learners' grammar, as we mentioned earlier.

As to the results on the grammaticality judgment tasks, the Spanish stimulus sentence that provoked the most empty COMP responses from the Francophones was also an instance of preposition stranding. The distraction of the stranded preposition is quite likely to have influenced the Francophones' responses, for recall that in written translation these same subjects produced no empty COMPs in Spanish. The Anglophones, on the other hand, produced empty COMPs with non-preposition-stranding stimuli sentences also.

CONCLUSIONS

To summarize, we have suggested that the acquisition of some fairly subtle differences between related languages has no straightforward unidimensional explanation. We have found that transfer, universal grammar, and learner-produced hypotheses all interact in shaping the emerging learner grammar. We also have isolated some cases where the learner's intake of the TL structure is initially shaped by superficial, and sometimes only apparent, similarities with the NL. Since the learner's intake is NL-shaped, it is clear that the hypotheses developed on the basis of this intake may lead the learner grammar away, rather than toward, the TL. Thus the task faced by learners of even a nonnative language closely related to their own is quite impressive. A more refined linguistic analysis of the systems to be learned and the system being learned leads to an interactive multifaceted view of the language learning process. As we use more sophisticated models of language structure and performance, clearer details of this interaction will be perceived, leading to more precise hypotheses for acquisition theory. In order to achieve this end, we need to develop detailed studies of subtle acquisition phenomena. Studies of this type will need to focus on learners in natural settings as well as classroom guided learners. The environment the learner is in will have a direct influence on the way in which the intake data are structured. Teaching may suggest possibilities that would not occur to the nonguided learner. A comparison of these different learners tackling the same acquisition problem will help us to focus on the mechanisms used by the learner and will more clearly develop useful hypotheses for acquisition theory.

APPENDIX

Sample Stimuli Sentences

The following are samples of the stimuli used in our tests.

[NP] in COMP
1. This is the professor *whom* we need.
2. Elle a photographié la fille *laquelle* tu aimes.
3. Esa es la profesora *quien* nosotros necesitamos aquí.

[PP] in COMP
4. This is the professor *to whom* I gave the book.
5. Tu verras le professeur *auquel* j'ai donné ces livres.
6. Busco a la chica *a quien* enviamos la carta.

Preposition stranding
7. Anna is the woman *that* I was in love *with* last year.
8. Demain tu verras le professeur *que* j'ai parlé *avec* chez Paul.
9. Este es el lápiz *que* escribo *con.*

Empty COMP
10. I am going to call the person _____ you want to see.
11. Je vais acheter le livre _____ tu veux.
12. Voy a llamar al chico _____ tú quieres ver.

Empty COMP + preposition stranding
13. I saw the film _____ you talked *about.*
14. Je connais bien l'étudiant _____ tu sortais *avec.*
15. Ana es la chica _____ Pedro vive *con.*

Doubly filled COMP: relatives
16. This is the professor *who that* we prefer.
17. J'ai rencontré la fille *laquelle que* tu cherchais.
18. Aquí está el libro *el cual que* nosotros buscábamos.

Doubly filled COMP: interrogatives
19. John says *who that* teaches math.
20. Antoine demande *où que* tu vas.
21. Juan pregunta *que quién* habla español aquí.

NOTES

1. Research for this project was supported by a grant from the Humanities Research Fund of the University of Ottawa to Adjémian. The authors wish to express their gratitude to the following student assistants for their help in the experimental tasks and in the editing process: Renée Corbeil, Margaret Murphy, Rosario Vidosa, and especially Manuel S. Belmonte.

2. For English see Chomsky and Lasnik 1977; for French, see Kayne 1976; for Spanish, see Rivero 1979.

3. The deletion of a PP in COMP is also normally excluded. Dropping a preposition would violate the principle of recoverability of deletion, a principle that is relevant to more than the syntax of relative clauses. Compare: The man you spoke to/ the man to whom you spoke/ *the man you spoke.

4. *Que* → *qui* / _____ *t* VP.

5. We shall qualify this statement for French later.

6. Unless otherwise stated, all filters we discuss affect the COMP nodes. We therefore omit labeling of the filter brackets for the sake of visual simplicity.

7. [e] is an empty COMP. We assume that *dont* and *où* can be analyzed as PPs in French.

8. Note that this does not mean the elementary level for English and French. Most students at the University of Ottawa have had some experience, albeit not formal exposure, to French and English.

9. One way of testing their possible perception of *quien* as a complementizer like *qui* is in *that* -trace extraction configurations. If they permit *quien* in such configurations, then clearly they do not perceive it as *who*. We study this and related matters in Adjémian and Liceras (in progress).

10. There were no preposition-stranding stimuli materials in French and Spanish, since these languages do not behave like English with respect to this phenomenon. We do not give figures for the results from the oral tasks on PPs in COMP, as our stimuli were too few and too difficult to give any interesting results.

11. See van Riemsdijk (1979) and Hornstein and Weinberg (1981).

12. Francophones produced no empty COMPs in translation into native language tasks, as one would expect, while Anglophones did. Interestingly our Anglophone subjects produced more empty COMPs in their native language in written than in oral translation, both when the stimuli to be translated were in Spanish and French.

13. Interestingly, the results from the repetition into Spanish L2 task and translation into target language task parallel in terms of percentage of empty COMPs produced what we saw in translation into native language tasks, where Anglophones use more empty COMPs in written translation into native language than in oral translation (see footnote 12). This might reflect the greater difficulty the learner has in parsing language in real time than in written form. In real time all available grammatical morphemes will aid in parsing; thus empty COMPs will be avoided.

9 Dative Questions and Markedness

Irene Mazurkewich
Université de Montréal

INTRODUCTION

One of the central aims of linguistic theory has been to provide an acquisitional model that has both descriptive and explanatory adequacy and will account for the fact that a child is able to acquire her/his maternal language given the well-recognized fact that primary input is impoverished or even "degenerate." A plausible acquisitional model has been proposed by Chomsky (cf. 1980, 1981a, 1981b, 1981c), who claims that a child approaches the language learning task equipped with a universal grammar (UG) which is posited to be a common biological endowment. UG provides the "core grammar" of a language determined by a restrictive system of principles; however, the parameters of individual languages are open in that they are set by experience obtained from the particular language a child is exposed to. It must be kept in mind that core grammar does not directly generate a language but rather, as Chomsky argues, it is an idealized construct that interacts with other properties of the human mind to generate a language. It is postulated within this theory that core grammar will be made up of relatively unmarked rules that are predicted to be easy to learn since they are part of UG and, futhermore, they could be learned on the basis of quite limited evidence. Marked rules, on the other hand, will be more difficult to learn because they are peripheral rules of core grammar. Moreover, they must be learned on the basis of positive evidence of their existence in the language as they could not be assumed a priori by the learner. Thus, markedness plays an important role in the language learning process because it makes predictions about the acquisitional sequence in real time. What is required, however, is a theory of markedness that will specify the structures that will be admitted to the core grammar. Using data gathered on the acquisition of dative questions by second language learners of English, it is our intention in this paper to argue for one of the parameters of the core grammar of English.[1]

BACKGROUND AND RATIONALE

The question of whether the learning processes in the acquisition of a first language are the same as those used in second language acquisition is still moot.

Many of the researchers debating this problem have concentrated on error analyses based on morpheme studies for evidence, and the finding of similarities in the types of errors made by first and second language learners has led some to postulate that the processes are essentially the same (Corder 1967, Dulay and Burt 1972, Richards 1971). Although the question remains open, we will adopt the same position for the case of dative questions. There are no studies reported in the literature that have focused on the acquisition of dative questions by native English children that we are aware of, so that we do not know precisely when they are learned or how. It appears that second language learners are not overtly taught these structures. If they were, some instructions would seem to be required specifically on how to strand prepositions so as to produce the type of dative question that is normally used, and there is no discussion in pedagogical materials of this kind that we have seen. Thus, we assume that second language learners acquire dative questions in much the same way that native speakers do.

Dative questions in English may take either of the alternative forms shown in 1 and 2:

1   a. To who(m) did Cathy give a book?
               b. For who(m) did Bill buy a present?
2   a. Who(m) did Cathy give a book to?
               b. Who(m) did Bill buy a present for?

The sentences in 1 demonstrate the phenomenon of "pied piping" in which the preposition has been fronted along with the *wh*-word. The sentences in 2 demonstrate the familiar case of preposition stranding in English. We suggest that the sentences in 1 represent the unmarked dative question form while those in 2 represent the marked one. There is some diachronic evidence to support our claim. Allen (1980), for example, reports that pied piping was obligatory for dative questions in Old English and that the stranding of prepositions in these cases took place at a later date. Also, van Riemsdijk (1978) claims that preposition stranding is a marked phenomenon which is rarely found in the languages of the world. For example, although preposition stranding is commonly found in English, it is less common in the Scandinavian languages (Allen 1980) and it occurs only in restricted cases involving the so-called *r*-words in Dutch (van Riemsdijk 1978), as well as in very restricted cases involving some prepositions in French (Vinet 1979). In the spoken language of contemporary English, dative questions in which the preposition is pied-piped along with the *wh*-word are seldom heard, and Ross (1968–1977) suggests that this structure has become extinct. It is still found, however, in the written form of the language. This means that unmarked dative question forms in English would rarely, if ever, be available in the linguistic environment that learners, either first or second, are exposed to. Nevertheless, in the theory of markedness we assume, the prediction is that the unmarked structure would be acquired before the marked one, and we tested this prediction using second language students from two unrelated language backgrounds—French and Inuktitut—who were learning English as a second language. The exposure to English of these two groups is quite different. The French students are taught English as a second language while their main education is carried out in French. The Inuit students, on the other hand, are educated mainly in English, but they receive instruction in Inuktitut throughout their primary and secondary school years. The students in this study who are from the eastern Arctic must, for instance, learn the syllabic writing system for their language, and this is started in the first grade before they begin to learn to write in English.

THE EXPERIMENTAL SUBJECTS AND PROCEDURE

It has been demonstrated that the acquisition of the dative alternation in declarative contexts is relatively late-learned in native English children (Fischer 1971, 1976; Roeper et al. 1981), and we assume that the acquisition of dative questions would also be learned late, although as mentioned earlier, there is no indication in the published literature of precisely when this is accomplished. Based on some preliminary investigations, we chose subjects who were at the high school or college levels for this study. The experimental groups were made up of 45 native French speakers whose average age was 18.0 years and 38 native Inuktitut speakers whose average age was 17.0 years. The subjects were classified as beginners (group 1), intermediate (group 2), and advanced (group 3) on the basis of the results of a cloze test that was carried out and which we used as an index to judge their level of achievement in English. We had two control groups of native English speakers. One group (Cont 1) was made up of 6 students who were in grade 7 and whose average age was 12.3 years, and a second group (Cont 2) that was made up of 6 students who were in grade 10 and whose average age was 15.6 years. We had originally started out with the younger Cont 1 group, because we had assumed that their acquisition of English syntactic structures would have been accomplished by this time, but on reconsideration of the kinds of tests which we were using, we decided to use a second group of native speakers, the Cont 2 group, who were closer in age and scholarship to the experimental groups. We found a variation in the results obtained from these two groups which may be due to developmental factors, and we therefore decided to report the results separately.

We investigated the acquisition of dative questions by means of an operational test which elicited the data in a written form. The subjects were provided with a series of declarative sentences and were asked to change them by questioning the underlined phrase. An example of a stimulus sentence used in this test is as follows:

3   Cathy gave a book *to Kevin*.

The subject's task was to question the phrase *to Kevin*. In order to make clear the nature of the task, they were given the following example:

4   John saw *Mary* last night.
                       Who(m) did John see last night?

We wanted to avoid influencing the responses elicited by questioning the indirect object; so we provided a sample sentence containing a direct object whose questioning does not involve the use of prepositions. Since the use of *who* or *whom* depends in part on the dialect of the speaker and since it was possible that our subjects, as second language learners, had been taught that there was a distinction between the two, we incorporated both forms in our testing by using *who(m)*. However, they were told that both forms were acceptable to relieve them of any doubts they might have had. The test sentences contain *to-* and *for-*dative verbs that optionally permit the dative alternation and verbs that obligatorily take prepositional phrase complements. One set of stimulus sentences contains five *to-*dative verbs—*give, lend, read, send,* and *throw*—that optionally permit the alternation, and three *to-*dative verbs—*explain, report,* and *suggest*—that obligatorily take prepositional phrase complements. A parallel set of stimulus sentences containing five *for-*dative verbs that optionally permit the alternation—*bake, buy, choose, make,* and *save*—and three *for-*dative verbs that obligatorily take prepositional phrase complements—*capture, create,* and *design*—were also tested. We included as well a set of distractor stimulus sentences containing the following verbs—*annoy, chase, rescue, take,* and *walk*—and which do not contain dative structures. The stimulus sentences are classified as follows:

Type 1: These sentences contain dative verbs that optionally permit the dative alternation, and the dative NP appears in a prepositional phrase:

5
    a. Peter threw a football *to Phillip.*
    b. Diane baked a cake *for Nicole.*

Type 2: These sentences contain dative verbs that optionally permit the dative alternation, and the dative NP appears as the first NP of a double-NP complement:

6
    a. Peter threw *Phillip* a football.
    b. Diane baked *Nicole* a cake.

Type 3: These sentences contain dative verbs that obligatorily take prepositional phrase complements, and the dative NP appears in this form:

7
    a. David suggested a trip *to Ruth.*
    b. Paul designed a house *for Claire.*

Type 4: These are distractor sentences which do not contain dative structures:

8
    a. Fred took *Joanne* to a movie.
    b. Andrew chased *Richard* upstairs.

In sentence types 1 to 3, the subjects and indirect objects are [+animate] and the direct objects are [−animate] and they are both full noun phrases rather than pronominal ones. The verbs which permit the alternation are typically monosyllabic, while the verbs which do not permit the alternation are typically polysyllabic.[2] The sentences were randomized and the subjects were allowed to work at their own pace. A copy of the test used is shown in the Appendix.

CLASSIFICATION OF RESPONSES AND DISCUSSION OF RESULTS

The responses obtained in this testing were classified into six categories which were not determined a priori but seemed to be the minimum required in order to best characterize them for analysis. These categories are defined as follows:

Marked structures refer to responses in which the preposition has been stranded, as in:

9
    a. Who(m) did Peter throw a football to?
    b. Who(m) did Diane bake a cake for?

Unmarked structures refer to responses in which the preposition has been pied-piped along with the *wh*-word, as in:

10
    a. To who(m) did Peter throw a football?
    b. For who(m) did Diane bake a cake?

Double prepositions refer to responses containing two prepositions, as in:

11
    a. To who(m) did Peter throw a football to?
    b. For who(m) did Diane bake a cake for?

Echo refers to responses in which echo questions were elicited, as in:

12
    a. Peter threw who(m) a football?
    b. Diane baked who(m) a cake?

Who(m) refers to responses in which the preposition was omitted, as in:

13
    a. Who(m) did Peter throw a football?
    b. Who(m) did Diane bake a cake?

Nonclassifiable refers to responses that did not fall into any of the above categories. The most common examples of this category were responses in which it was usually the subject that was questioned, as in:

14
    a. Who threw a football?
    b. Who baked a cake?

Percentages of the total responses for the six categories described above were calculated for the control groups and for each of the three levels of the experimental groups. The results are given in Table 1.

The results of this testing indicate that the experimental subjects are well on their way to learning dative questions in English.[3] The Exp-I groups are more advanced in their acquisitional process in comparison with the Exp-F groups, but

Table 1. Distribution of Responses of Dative Questions, in Percentages

	Cont 1 (N=6)	Cont 2 (N=6)	Exp-F			Exp-I		
			1(N=23)	2(N=7)	3(N=15)	1(N=12)	2(N=8)	3(N=18)
Type 1: Peter threw a football *to Philip.*								
Marked st.	76.6	53.4	5.0	14.3	18.7	46.7	42.5	49.5
Unmarked st.	16.7	43.3	27.0	22.9	40.0	11.6	17.5	25.8
Double prep.	6.7	3.3			1.3	8.3	2.5	7.9
Echo			1.8			5.0	7.5	5.6
Who			66.2	48.5	40.0	26.7	27.5	6.7
Nonclass.				14.3		1.7	2.5	4.5
Type 2: Peter threw *Philip* a football.								
Marked st.	83.3	66.6	4.3	5.7	16.0	33.3	62.5	40.4
Unmarked st.	6.7	20.0	14.1	8.6	18.7	8.3	12.5	18.0
Double prep.		6.7				8.3	2.5	5.6
Echo			1.6			5.0	5.0	13.5
Who	6.7	6.7	80.0	80.0	65.3	41.8	12.5	16.9
Nonclass.	3.3			5.7		3.3	5.0	5.6
Type 3: David suggested the trip *to Ruth.*								
Marked st.	83.3	61.1	4.1	9.5	20.0	36.1	41.7	38.9
Unmarked st.	16.7	33.3	19.1	19.0	40.0	19.4	16.7	22.3
Double prep.						5.6	4.2	11.0
Echo								16.6
Who			75.3	52.4	40.0	36.1	29.2	9.3
Nonclass.		5.6	1.5	19.0		2.8	8.3	1.9
Type 4: Dennis annoyed *Karen* yesterday.								
Marked st.								
Unmarked st.								
Double prep.								
Echo						3.3	2.5	11.2
Who	100	100	97.5	91.4	100	93.4	95.0	85.4
Nonclass.			2.5	8.6		3.3	2.5	3.4

	Cont 1 (N=6)	Cont 2 (N=6)	Exp-F			Exp-I		
			1(N=23)	2(N=7)	3(N=15)	1(N=12)	2(N=8)	3(N=18)
Type 1: Diane baked a cake *for Nicole.*								
Marked st.	70.0	63.3	5.9	2.9	12.0	36.6	55.0	39.4
Unmarked st.	16.7	36.7	30.7	28.6	42.7	10.0	15.0	25.8
Double prep.	10.0					13.3		11.2
Echo	3.3		2.6			1.7	5.0	12.4
Who			60.8	57.1	45.3	31.7	25.0	9.0
Nonclass.				11.4		6.7		2.2
Type 2: Diane baked *Nicole* a cake.								
Marked st.	76.6	70.0	3.4	5.7	9.4	41.6	62.5	41.6
Unmarked st.	6.7	16.7	14.7	11.4	21.4	5.0	7.5	21.4
Double prep.	6.7					5.0		1.1
Echo		3.3	0.9			6.7	5.0	10.1
Who	10.0	3.3	77.3	71.5	69.2	40.0	20.0	19.1
Nonclass.		6.7	3.7	11.4		1.7	5.0	6.7

Table 1 (continued)

	Type 3: Paul designed a house *for Claire.*						
Marked st.	72.2	38.9	4.2	9.5	13.3	41.7	41.5	44.4
Unmarked st.	22.2	61.1	23.6	28.6	46.7	11.1	20.9	16.7
Double prep.						11.1		5.6
Echo	5.6		2.9				4.2	18.5
Who			69.3	47.6	40.0	36.1	29.2	11.1
Nonclass.				14.3			4.2	3.7

this is probably because, as mentioned above, their exposure to English is quite different. Furthermore, the results indicate that the subjects from both experimental groups seem to be more advanced in their acquisition of *to*-dative verbs than *for*-dative verbs. This tendency, suggesting that there is a later acquisition for *for*-datives, showed up consistently in other tests that were carried out (cf. Mazurkewich 1981), and a similar finding was reported by Fischer (1971) in her investigation of the acquisition of dative structures by young native English children. It may be that *for*-datives are more complex to acquire than *to*-datives, and therefore are acquired later, because *to*-datives usually involve notions of transference while *for*-datives involve notions of benefactiveness that, as Goldsmith (1980) points out, can be quite vague and as a result are broad in coverage.

The data suggest that the experimental subjects learn dative questions by first using the pronoun *who(m)* without a preposition, a structure in which the grammatical function of the indirect object pronoun is not differentiated from that of the direct object. It is entirely possible that some subjects were influenced in performing this task by the example they were offered, but the results indicate that this would have been the case only with the subjects who were classified as beginners since there is a progressive decrease in the use of the bare *who(m)* elicited from the intermediate and advanced groups. The results also clearly indicate that the experimental groups learn the unmarked form of dative questions first and master the marked ones later.[4] This acquisitional sequence obtains even though, as mentioned earlier, it is the marked and not the unmarked structure that would be available in the linguistic environment that learners are exposed to. This sequence is more easily seen in the results obtained from the Exp-F groups who consistently produced higher percentages of unmarked questions in comparison with marked ones. Although the Exp-I groups produced higher percentages of marked structures, reflecting the fact that they are further advanced in their acquisition of English, they also produced progressively higher percentages of unmarked structures, which lends support to our claim that it is the latter structure which is acquired first. The developmental sequence is not clear-cut, however, because both the experimental intermediate groups, group 2, tend to demonstrate an indeterminacy effect which also showed up in other testing that was carried out. The fact that there are fewer subjects in this group as compared with the beginner and advanced groups may also be responsible to some extent for this variability.

It may be argued that the Exp-F groups acquire the unmarked dative question structures first using the strategy of straight transference of a similar structure from French to English; however, the acquisitional sequence of the unmarked structures demonstrated by the Inuit subjects would rule out this explanation. Inuktitut is a polysynthetic language in which nouns are case marked, word order is relatively free, and there are no prepositions. Thus the data indicate that both experimental groups acquire dative questions in the same way, and we suggest that this learning process is governed by linguistic universals rather than other factors such as transference.

On another level of abstraction, the acquisitional sequence obtained in this testing is consistent with the notion of markedness outlined within the framework of case theory, such as that proposed by Chomsky (1981a). In this framework, all lexical nouns in English must be assigned case, and this assignment takes place at S-structure, that is, the level after movement rules have applied. In the unmarked option, case is assigned by the verb or a preposition to an adjacent noun phrase; thus dative questions as in 10a and b would be considered the unmarked ones. The problem arises with the assignment of case in stranded questions such as 9a and b. They require a special rule that learners would have to acquire on the basis of positive evidence of their existence in the language, since stranding, as mentioned earlier, is a marked phenomenon that is rarely found in other languages. The necessity for a rule to derive the stranded structure would therefore relegate the latter to the marked periphery of the core grammar of English under the analysis assumed here.[5]

THE LEARNING OF PREPOSITION STRANDING

In order to produce the marked structure form of dative questions, learners must know how to strand prepositions. The category we have labeled "double prepositions," shown in 11a and b, suggests the learning strategy used here is a mnemonic one. In other words, it seems that the learner starts with an already acquired unmarked structure placing the dative prepositional phrase at the front of the sentence concomitantly with a copied preposition in the stranded position. The stranded preposition acts like a linguistic quipu marking the position in surface structure in which it appears in the underlying structure. Once the learner internalizes the linking or coindexing of the wh-phrase to its underlying position, the fronted preposition becomes redundant so that it is no longer copied and a marked structure results. The pronoun who(m) is not copied in the stranded position because the subjects already know how to front wh-words, but with dative questions that involve wh-phrases, it is the preposition-stranding phenomenon that must be learned. The fact that the younger subjects in the

Cont 1 group produced more double prepositions than the older Cont 2 subjects did suggests that this may well be a developmental strategy used as well by native speakers to facilitate their learning of preposition stranding. The Exp-I subjects show a greater reliance on this strategy in comparison with the Exp-F subjects, but this "overgeneration" may be related to the lack of prepositions in their maternal language, which might create greater difficulty for the Inuit in learning English prepositions than it does for the French.[6] It may also be that the Exp-F subjects rely less on this strategy in English because they already know how to strand prepositions, as stranding is permitted with certain prepositions in the Québecois dialect these subjects are exposed to.[7] For example, utterances of the following type:

15   la fille que j'ai sorti avec[8]
16   le boss que je travaille pour

which allow prepositional stranding, are found in this dialect.

THE GRAMMATICAL STATUS OF PREPOSITIONLESS DATIVE QUESTIONS

In type 2 stimulus sentences which contain double-NP complements, the first NP, the dative NP, takes the structural position usually occupied by the direct object. Thus, if the first NP in a sentence such as 6a, repeated here as 17a, is questioned, it would derive 17b:

17   a. Peter threw *Phillip* a football.
                             b. Who(m) did Peter throw a football?

The grammatical status of questions such as 17b has provoked much discussion in the literature (cf. Fillmore 1965, Ross 1967, Kuroda 1968, Hankamer 1973, Langendoen et al. 1973). Fillmore and Ross consider sentences such as 17b to be ungrammatical, but Langendoen et al. claim to have found some speakers for whom such sentences are grammatical.[9] However, there is a serious drawback in their experimental design. In one test, their subjects were asked to answer questions using complete sentences, but in the stimulus sentences used to elicit a reply to dative questions, the prepositions were omitted; for example:

18   a. Who did you offer the man?
                             b. Who did you give the ball?

Clearly the authors did not want to reveal the grammatical status of the *wh*-phrases but, as Hornstein and Weinberg (1981) point out, even if their subjects consider such questions to be ungrammatical, they are nevertheless perfectly answerable. Using an intuitive judgment test to elicit data on sentences of this type, it was demonstrated that our native English-speaking control subjects generally found them to be ungrammatical (Mazurkewich 1981). Attempts to rule out these kinds of sentences by applying, for example, derivational constraints on the first NP of a double-NP construction have been proposed by Kuroda (1968), but they were shown to be inadequate by Oehrle (1976). However, some sort of constraint is needed for these cases, and in order to illustrate this point we will look at an example discussed by Oehrle (1976) in which it seems to be freely permitted. Oehrle argues convincingly that the dative alternation in English is best accounted for by a lexical rather than a transformational rule. Thus, dative verbs that permit both prepositional phrase and double-NP complements have both subcategorial features in the base. He claims, furthermore, that there are particular readings that are available only from sentences containing double-NP complements. For example, Oehrle argues that the following sentence:

19   Nixon gave Mailer the book.

is ambiguous, since one reading asserts that the ownership of the book passed from Nixon to Mailer while another is compatible with a situation in which Mailer was handed the book by Nixon and questions of ownership are irrelevant. He suggests that there is also a third possible reading that involves a "causal" relationship that is compatible with a situation in which Mailer wrote a book that he would not have been able to write if it had not been for Nixon but that this reading can be obtained only from the sentence containing the double-NP complement. It is not available in the related sentence which has the prepositional phrase complement:

20   Nixon gave the book to Mailer.

If the indirect object is questioned, for example:

21   Who(m) did Nixon give the book to?

only the reading of transference and not causality is obtained. Similarly, verbs that denote inalienable property obligatorily require double-NP complements, as the following examples demonstrate:

22   a. Pat gave Mike a kick.
                            b. Pat gave Mike a black eye.
23   a. *Pat gave a kick to Mike.
                            b. *Pat gave a black eye to Mike.

In this case, the questioning of the first NP of the double-NP complements in 22 a and b would derive ungrammatical questions:

24   a. *Who(m) did Pat give a kick to?
                            b. *Who(m) did Pat give a black eye to?

These facts quite clearly indicate that the first NP of the double-NP complement of dative verbs cannot be moved out by rule of *wh*-movement. This constraint does not apply to echo questions in which the first NP is questioned in situ which are grammatical. Rather, the problem arises with the movement of dative NPs from this position, and this is what must be accounted for in spite of the fact that there is no problem in comprehending ungrammatical utterances, such as 17b and 18a and b, in which the prepositions have been omitted.

Proposals involving perceptual or parsing strategies that look for "gaps" in analyzing dative questions have been made by Jackendoff and Culicover (1971), Otsu (1977), Fodor (1978), Fodor and Frazier (1980), as well as Wanner and Maratsos (1978) who have developed an augmented transition network (ATN) model for the syntactic processing of sentences. In Fodor's model, for example, the gap following the preposition would be a doubtless one while the gap following the verb would be a doubtful one. However, if our analysis is correct, there would not be a gap at all following the verb that could be related to the first NP of a double-NP complement, so that this would not present a problem for gapping strategies in general.

Proposals have also been made by linguists working within the framework of case theory to suggest how the grammar would be constrained so that prepositionless datives would not be derived (cf. Chomsky 1981a; Hornstein and Weinberg 1981; Stowell 1981, 1982). Stowell, for example, suggests that the first NP of a double-NP complement, as in 17a, is incorporated within the subphrasal structure of the verbal head to form a "syntactic word" (*threw Phillip*), and the second NP (*a football*), would be assigned case, as it would then be adjacent to the verb. Since the transformational rule "move α" cannot analyze the substructure of a syntactic word, the verbal phrase (*threw Phillip*) in this instance, the dative NP *Phillip* would not be accessible to this rule, thereby accounting for the fact that prepositionless dative questions would not be generated by the grammar.

Our claim that the first NP of the double-NP complement of dative verbs cannot be extracted by a movement rule appears to be immediately falsified by the data elicited using type 2 stimulus sentences. We suggest that when the issue is forced, as it was here, the subjects simply make use of the knowledge they have already acquired for questioning indirect objects in prepositional phrases and apply it in this case as well. This seems plausible, especially since they show no difficulty in recognizing the grammatical relations of the NP complements involved and it does not appear to occur to them a priori that it is not possible.

In conclusion, by concentrating on a case in point, the acquisition of dative questions by second language learners of English, we have provided evidence in support of a theory of markednesss and shown how it mediated the language acquisition process. The data bear out the prediction that the unmarked dative question structure is acquired before the marked one in spite of the fact that the unmarked form may only be minimally available to learners in the linguistic input they receive. Furthermore, we have argued that this acquisition sequence is consistent with the theory of case that has been proposed recently.

APPENDIX

Change the following declarative sentences into questions by replacing the italicized phrase with either "*who*" or "*whom,*" depending on how you would say it in ordinary conversation. An example would be as follows:

John saw *Mary* last night.	Who did John see last night?

1. Diane baked *Nicole* a cake.
2. David suggested the trip *to Ruth.*
3. Isabel made a sweater *for Jerry.*
4. Dennis annoyed *Karen* yesterday.
5. Paul designed a house *for Claire.*
6. Sylvia chose *Betty* a pattern.
7. Peter threw a football *to Philip.*
8. Cathy gave *Kevin* a book.
9. Allen lent a dollar *to Louise.*
10. Bill bought *Mary* a present.
11. Tom captured the prize *for Canada.*
12. Jack read *Kim* a story.
13. Diane baked a cake *for Nicole.*
14. Bill bought a present *for Mary.*
15. Patrick rescued *Lisa* from drowning.
16. Nancy saved a seat *for Mark.*
17. Fred took *Joanne* to a movie.
18. Anne created a costume *for Sara.*
19. Cathy gave a book *to Kevin.*
20. Bob reported the accident *to the police.*
21. Isabel made *Jerry* a sweater.
22. John sent a postcard *to Carol.*
23. Andrew chased *Richard* upstairs.
24. Sylvia chose a pattern *for Betty.*
25. Peter threw *Philip* a football.
26. Allen lent *Louise* a dollar.
27. Sam walked *Muriel* home from school.
28. John sent *Carol* a postcard.
29. Nancy saved *Mark* a seat.
30. Jack read a story *to Kim.*

1. _____ ?
2. _____ ?
3. _____ ?
4. _____ ?
5. _____ ?
6. _____ ?
7. _____ ?
8. _____ ?
9. _____ ?
10. _____ ?
11. _____ ?
12. _____ ?
13. _____ ?
14. _____ ?
15. _____ ?
16. _____ ?
17. _____ ?
18. _____ ?
19. _____ ?
20. _____ ?
21. _____ ?
22. _____ ?
23. _____ ?
24. _____ ?
25. _____ ?
26. _____ ?
27. _____ ?
28. _____ ?
29. _____ ?
30. _____ ?

NOTES

1. I would like to thank Rajendra Singh and Alison d'Anglejan for their help and advice. This research was supported by a grant from the Ministère de l'Education du Québec (FCAC) to A. d'Anglejan et al. for which I am grateful. I thank as well Elly van Gelderen, Anne Grafstein, and Alan Bailin for their sagacious comments.
2. There are polysyllabic dative verbs, e.g., *promise, guarantee, assign, allow,* which are exceptions to the morphological constraint as they permit double-NP complements. Verbs of this kind were not used in this testing.
3. We have included echo questions since they are perfectly grammatical responses. However, the analysis of such questions involves principles such as intonation which are quite apart from the ones we are concerned with here. We list them as a separate category because we did not

want to obscure the percentages of grammatical responses that were elicited, but we shall not have anything further to say about them.

4. In transformational generative grammar the prepositional phrase would be moved to the front of the sentence by the general rule "move α" and the redundant preposition would result from a spelling out of trace. In a base-generated theory, such as the one outlined by Koster (1978), the wh-phrase which appears at the beginning of the sentence in surface structure would be linked by a coindexing rule to its underlying position which would be an empty category; thus the spelling out of the redundant preposition would result from the copying of a prepositional consequent. With respect to dative questions in an active context, at least, both theories are able to account for these sentences. In the case of dative questions in a passive context, the theoretical analyses differ in important ways. This point is discussed in detail in Mazurkewich (1981).

5. The special rule needed here may involve that of reanalysis as suggested by Hornstein and Weinberg (1981); however, there have been other proposals made by linguists working within the theories of case, government, and binding. For a more detailed discussion on this point, see Chomsky (1981a, Chap. 5) and the sources cited here.

6. In other testing involving stimulus sentences that elicited dative questions in a passive context, we found that a higher percentage of responses containing double prepositions were produced not only by the native Inuktitut and French speakers but by the younger control group of native English speakers as well (Mazurkewich 1981). Dative questions in a passive context seem to be a very difficult structure to acquire in general, and some of our subjects appear to make more use of the double preposition learning strategy for its acquisition.

7. Vinet (1979) reports that preposition stranding is found in other varieties of French spoken around the world.

8. In this nonstandard Québecois dialect, *sortir* is conjugated with the auxiliary verb *avoir* and not with *être*.

9. There does not seem to be variability of grammaticality judgments in the case of *for*-dative prepositionless questions, as in :

(i)   *Who did Diane bake a cake?
(ii)   *Who did Bill buy a present?

as they seem to be considered ungrammatical in general. However, there are many *to*-dative questions of this type that seem to be ungrammatical as well, for example:

(iii)   *Who did John read the story?
(iv)   *Who did Anne write the letter?
(v)   *Who did Bob sell the car?

In fact, it looks as if ambiguous judgments of prepositionless dative questions concern only a few dative verbs, and they appear to be the most commonly used ones.

10 Temporal Systems and Universality in Interlanguage: A Case Study

Lorraine Kumpf
UCLA

Interlanguage has been thought of as systematic for many years, and its systematicity has been approached from many perspectives. In the acquisition of grammatical morphology, analyses have often assumed that the categories of the interlanguage are the same as the target language: all the "morpheme studies" make this assumption. In addition, the grammatical categories of the native language have been assumed to be part of the interlanguage: studies in transfer are exemplary. What is virtually missing is an approach which treats interlanguage as systematic in and of itself, as sets of grammatical relationships which have been established by the speaker. This approach necessitates discovering the speaker's system without reference to the grammatical categories of the native or target languages; it seems to me to be the most basic way in which we can understand the grammar of interlanguages. In the present analysis, a certain kind of interlanguage is described independently of the target or native language categories. This case study will show that interlanguage reflects discourse structure and relates to universals in ways that other natural languages do.

The viewpoint taken here, the "discourse-functional" approach, applies to both native language and interlanguage analysis. Although both terms have various associations in linguistics and in second language acquisition, I mean them in a very transparent sense. The use of a form is indexed to a particular context in discourse. Interpretations of morphological or syntactic structures are always given in terms of the occurrence of forms in actual discourse. The assumption is that any grammatical form appears to fulfill a function in the discourse: it is the discourse context which creates the conditions under which the forms appear, and in order to explain the forms, it is necessary to refer to this context.

The approach is perhaps easier to see for native language discourse, in which speakers control a range of possible structures for a given context, and "choose" to present certain ones for certain purposes. I claim that the same assumption can be made for interlanguage discourse. Although the same range of possibilities may not be open to second language speakers, it is assumed that if communication is consistently achieved, then regular relationships between form and function do indeed exist. Given this assumption, we can discover system in interlanguages by looking at the discourse contexts which yield the forms.

We can start with what is known about the structure of discourse. Conversation and narrative exist as basic discourse modes in every natural language. Narrative is of particular interest here, as the best source for revealing tense and aspect relationships. Narrative is by definition a story line, and in any story, the line of even clauses, which I will call the *foreground*, can be contrasted with those clauses which elaborate on the even line, clauses which I will call the *background*. These terms have been used in grammatical analyses such as Hopper (1979) and Givón (1982); they originate from the gestalt psychologists' notion of figure and ground perception. The foreground, then, is the event line, and the background consists of clauses which set the scene, make digressions, change the normal sequence of events, or give evaluative remarks. For virtually any language which has been described in this regard, the background is more elaborate in terms of temporal grammatical devices than the foreground. The background marking load is greater—in whatever way the language does that—because there is more to explain, in terms of time relationships. Contrast the event line, which stays in the same time frame for the entire episode or story.

In addition to using narrative to reveal tense and aspect, it is necessary to look at conversation, which by its nature shows modality variety, in such characteristic speech events as questioning, demanding, stating preferences, desires, and abilities. Of course, conversation also manifests tense and aspect, but in a less structured way than narrative. Conversation abounds in irrealis forms, that is, verb forms in other than real time. These two basic modes of discourse should go far in revealing the tense-aspect-modality relations in interlanguages.

The type of subject used here may be very important to the analysis. The subject has learned English-based interlanguage by contact, in untutored situations. In addition, she has stopped acquiring, although she continues to use her interlanguage on a daily basis. These characteristics are shared by other interlanguage speakers I have studied, who use this language to varying degrees, depending on the purpose it serves in their daily lives as immigrants. For these speakers, their own form of the target has been internalized. That is, these speakers have created systematic grammatical relations and internalized them, regularizing the input to their own norms. These regularities have become stable as they have fossilized. The degree and quality of this internal regularization is the question which underlies this analysis.

I note in passing that opinions differ on the extent to which classroom instruction influences the spontaneous discourse of second language speakers. Although there may be little or no influence, I want to assure no intervention of this variable by analyzing untutored speech. The question of identifying input is of course unsolved, and presents a problem for drawing conclusions about the speakers' modes of acquisition.

The method of analysis is as follows. Clauses of continuous discourse were coded according to the points listed below. Through the resulting counts, it is possible to show how discourse structures correlate with a semantic characterization of aspect, with verb types, verb forms, clause types, and so on.

Coding points

1   *Discourse structure*
           conversation/narrative
           foreground/background
           episode boundary

2   *Semantic reference—aspect*
           completive/noncompletive
           continuous action
           habitual (action or state)
           anterior

3   *Verb types*
           transitive/intransitive
           active/stative

4   *Verb forms*
           base
           WAS Verb+IN
           Verb +IN
           "irregular past"/invariant form
           copula
           Verb +ED
           nonfinite verb
           modal

5   *Clause types*
           subordinate
           embedded
           clause without overt verb
           clause without subject/topic
           clause without subject/topic, verb
           interrogative
           imperative
           negative
           other irrealis

6   *Time reference*
           present time
           past time
           future time

7   *Other*
           chunks, routines
           repetitions

In the above, the categories for time reference, aspectual reference, discourse structure, verb type, and clause type are considered "universal"—representing things which can be done in any language. The designation of verb type and semantic reference are approximations based on the meaning of the whole clause; the other categories are more easily considered discrete. For this analysis, I am defining the term *foreground* as any clause that pushes the event line forward, and *background* as any clause that does not. This effectively avoids the circularity involved in interpreting the verb form in terms of the narrative and the narrative function in terms of the verb form.

The case presented here is that of a Japanese speaker, Tomiko, who came to the United States in 1952 as the bride of an American serviceman who was fluent in both spoken and written Japanese. She came with no English, and was left alone for long periods to get along with neighbors and in-laws, none of whom spoke Japanese. She is gregarious and an excellent communicator. At the time of the taping, she had been in the United States for 28 years, and was very fluent in her interlanguage, which nevertheless remained nonnative-like in verb marking. An ordinary semantic analysis based on the categories of English would yield little regularity in her temporal system; however, when the data from her long narrative monologues are broken down in terms of discourse structure, a system becomes clearer.

A sample of narrative text follows. The foreground clauses are underlined. The first four clauses are scene-setting. The third clause represents "anterior" reference; here, the past of past. Notice that clause 7, *door was flyin open*, is designated foreground. Even though, as we shall see, it is the only clause so designated which uses the WAS Verb+IN form, this clause seems to push the line of events forward, that is, to be "what happens next." In the static, descriptive background, the verb WAS and the form WAS Verb+IN predominate. In line 21, the seeing is the foreground event, and what was seen is in the background, in an embedded clause. That same foreground/background relationship is found in line 28, of ther verb *say* to what is said. It is conceivable, however, that the line of events be forwarded in an embedded clause. In line 27 we find a negative, which I have labeled background, since there is no event movement here. It is debatable whether negation, as nonaction, can ever be foreground, and certainly part of the reason that we choose to express something in the negative, rather than using some affirmative counterpart, is that we want to relegate the information to the background. But it must be allowed that negatives can indeed move the event line forward, by giving the nonaction an event status.

Text from Tomiko (foregrounded clauses italicized)
First time Tampa have a tornado come to.
Was about seven forty-five.
Bob go to work,
n I was inna bathroom
5 *and ... a ... tornado come*
shake everything.

Door was flyin open,
I was scared.
Hanna was sittin in window . . .
10 Hanna is a little dog.
French poodle.
I call Baby.
Anyway, she never wet bed,
she never wet anywhere.
15 But she was so scared
an cryin,
run to the bathroom,
come to me,
an she tinkle, tinkle, tinkle all over me. (laugh)
20 She was so scared.
I see somebody throwin a brick onna trailer
wind was blowin so hard
ana light . . . outside street light was on
oh I was really scared.
25 *An den second stop* ("and then in a second it stopped")
So I try to open door
I could not open
I say, "Oh, my God. What's happen?"
I look window // awning was gone.

Returning to the text, note that in line 26, tightly bound complement relations such as *try to open* were counted as single clauses. This excerpt is very typical of the text: most of the background consists of description with the marking characteristics shown here.

The results of the analysis of Tomiko's temporal system are given in Tables 1 through 4. First, the foregrounded clauses are given in Table 1. The base form is regularly used when expressing foreground events. The only noticeable exception is the use of forms such as *met, bought,* and *told*—the "irregular past" forms. It is difficult to tell the status of these forms, which may be learned as separate lexical items, because the nonpast counterparts of most of them do not come up in the text: it is impossible to say whether these forms are invariants. Clearly, however, the generalization is that completed action in the foreground is expressed with the base form.

Table 1. Foregrounded Clauses (Tomiko)

Verb form	%	Count	Example
Base	78.2	61	move, come, say, climb, look, make, run, work, wave, put
"Irregular past"	15.4	12	tol(d) $\times$ 2, done $\times$ 2, went, thought, heard, seen, met, got marry, bought
Verb + IN	5.1	4	jugglin, pushin, pullin, diggin
WAS Verb + IN	1.3	1	was flyin
Total foregrounded clauses		78	

In Table 2 we see the results of a count of the main clauses of the background. Note that most of the backgrounded clauses are stative and descriptive, for example:

I was scared
awning was gone

Table 2.   Backgrounded Clauses—Main (Tomiko)

Discourse-semantic function	Verb form	Verb type	% of total background	Count
A. Description, evaluation	Tensed*	Stative	39.5	68
Description, evaluation	No overt { subject / topic } or verb		7.6	13
Description, evaluation	No overt verb (copula)		3.5	6
Total			50.6	87
B. Description, continuous action	WAS Verb + IN	Active		12
Continuous action	Verb + IN	Active		5
Present habitual action	Base	Active		6
Past habitual action (or state)	USETA Verb /jùst ə/	Active, stative		5
Past habitual action	Verb + IN	Active		2
	Base	Active		1
Anterior ("pluperfect")	Base	Active		3
Anterior (past or present relevance)	BEEN Verb + IN	Active		1
Total			20.3	35
C. Irrealis				
Future	GONNA Verb	Active, stative		6
Imperative	Base	Active		1
Interrogative (wh only)	(follows above marking)	Active, stative		5
Negative	{ did / could / can } not V	Active, stative		12
Modals (auxiliaries) (except USETA)	{ can / could / haveta } V	Active, stative		10
Total irrealis and modals (some clauses overlap)			15.1	26

*See breakdown of statives, Table 4.

Some continuous-action clauses also function to describe or set the scene:

>wind was blowin
>rain was pourin down
>Hanna was sittin in window

Other continuous-action clauses report actions rather than describing scenes:

>I was walkin around
>picking up limb
>we diggin and diggin

The Verb+IN form can also express past habituality, as in

>every weekend drinkin, watchin TV,

but the usual form for past habitual action is /jústə/ (USETA) with the base form:[1]

>we useta go there
>I useta ride.

Incidental occurrences of other forms include the base form for the anterior "past-of-past" sense, and the BEEN Verb+IN form for the past-of-present-relevance sense. Table 2 also lists the irrealis/modality forms, none of which occur in great numbers. Table 3 shows "other" clauses, and reflects the fact that Tomiko is capable of producing embedded and subordinate clauses, although she rarely does. I call clauses such as *you name it, we got it* a "routine": Tomiko learned them as a unit but has only approximated the appropriate use. Here, the routine meant something like "we found anything and everthing there." Pronunciation of routines provides evidence that they are not "analyzed."

Tomiko's communicative abilities are reflected in the fact that she so rarely produced uninterpretable clauses. Although this intelligibility does not necessarily bring continuity in discourse, it obviously helps create effective communication. It is necessary to mention that intonation is an essential aspect of this intelligibility, and so is the assigning of clauses to discourse or form-related categories.

Table 4, is a breakdown of stative verbs and the tense marking shown in them, for main, affirmative background clauses. Note that almost 60 percent of

Table 3.   Other Clauses (Tomiko)

	Count
Embedded	7
Subordinated	6
Routines	3
Repetitions	2
Uninterpretable or ambiguous	6
Total	24*

*= 14% of total background

Table 4.   Stative Verb Tensing

	Count	% of statives
Statives showing tense		
copula	33	
VERB + ED	3	
GONNA VERB	3	
USETA VERB	1	
Total	40	58.8
Statives with indeterminant tensing		
"irregular past"	2	
present habituals	8	
Total	10	14.8
Stative invariant forms		
have	11	
wanna	7	
Total	18	24.6
% of statives showing tense including category 2	74	

all stative verbs are unambiguously tensed. The past tensing of some of the verbs with the -ed suffix shows that this form is known to the speaker, and this is an important point in claiming that the foreground/background distinction plays a role in the marking: that marked forms are needed in the background and not in the event line is the central generalization. The second category of statives is that whose tensing is indeterminant—the "irregular past" and the present habituals, which are not marked. If the viewpoint is taken that these forms are indeed tensed, then about 74 percent of the statives are marked. The third category is comprised of the forms HAVE and WANNA, which do not vary in any context. The form WANNA (and perhaps HAVE, as well) is close in form and meaning to a modal, and so interpreted, its invariance is easier to understand.

It is interesting to note that when the -IN form is used to report actions rather than to describe scenes, the WAS form is usually not present. So, for example, Tomiko says:

> we diggin junk out
> all people runnin around crazy
> somebody throwin brick onna trailer

This is in contrast to continuous forms which describe or set the scene, such as:

> wind was blowing
> rain was pourin down
> Hanna was sittin in window

Of course, the line between using the continuous to describe a scene and using it to report action is very fine: one might look at the action sentences above as scene-descriptive, too. However, this tendency is interesting because it supports the claimed relationship between stativity and tense marking. The fact is that the more stative the verb, the more likely it is to have the tense-carrying marker appear.

The clauses are totaled below in various ways. The first tally shows that the proportion of background to foreground is about two to one. This ratio undoubtedly varies from speaker to speaker and from story to story, in native as well as nonnative speech. In the second tally, the verb forms are broken down in terms of forms relative to background and foreground. The base form characterizes the foreground; the background manifests many forms, including those carrying aspectual distinctions, and especially, tense. Third, the percentages of forms marked for tense in the foreground and background are shown. Notice that tenses are rarely expressed in foreground, and even if the suppletive "past" forms are counted as tensed, only 16 percent are tensed. In the background, however, 63 percent of the clauses are unambiguously tensed, and if invariants are counted, over 80 percent are tensed. Background is the domain of tense. Fourth, percentages of tensing in selected verb categories are shown.

Totals from Tables

1. Foreground/background

	% of total	Count	
Foreground	31.2	78	
Background	68.8	172	
Total		250	total clauses

2. Verb form breakdown—Main clauses (in %)

	Base	WAS V+IN	V+IN	Copula	Invariant	V+ED	BEEN V+IN	"USETA" V
F	78.2	1.3	5.1		15.4			
B	18.5	12.2	7.1	33.6	18.5	3.0	1.0	6.1

3. Tenses marked (in %)

			If invariants considered "tensed"
F	1.3	or	16.7
B	63.0	or	81.5

4. Tensing of selected verbal categories

Category	Occurrences in tensed form (%)
Equation, attribute (copula)	100
Habitual past action/state	63
Continuous action	60

The copula, the most stative form, is tensed 100 percent of the time. The habitual past shows tense next more often, about 63 percent of the time, and the continuous follows with 60 percent. The other aspectual categories, all involving active verbs, are not regularly marked. This reflects the generalization that the more stative the verb, the more likely its tensing.

The conclusions from the data are:

1. Completed action in the foreground is expressed with the base verb form. There is no tensing of these verbs.
2. In the background are many marked forms, and most verbs are marked for tense, especially the stative verbs. Virtually all statives are tensed; active verbs in the background are marked for habitual and continuous aspect, and irregularly for tense.

The basic system is that tensing is not employed when referring to completed action. Tensing is employed when referring to states and to noncompleted action. In the background, there is variation yet to be accounted for, but it is clear that there are morphological correlates with the background/foreground distinction.

It is evident that this system can be looked upon as an interpretation of the English copula as tense carrier. Tomiko's acquisition of tense can be explained as a response to the salience of the copula. Although this viewpoint seems valid, it does not explain all the forms—for example, the existence of the Verb+ED forms in the background, or the marking not involving the copula. However, viewing the copula as tense carrier does not detract from looking at the system as presented here. This analysis simply shows how the system manifests itself in discourse, and it is this view that reveals the entire system best, including the special relationship between tensing and the copula.

Tomiko has created and internalized this system, which corresponds to neither the native nor the target language. Just as it is necessary to look at her language independently of the categories of English in order to arrive at a description of the system, it is necessary to view her tense-aspect system independently if we are able to relate it to what is known about temporal relationships in the discourse of other natural languages. Going on the initial assumption that the second language acquirer is using the same language-creating capacity that any acquirer does, we can assume that a system thus contrived and internalized will share the characteristics of temporal systems of other languages and conform to universals or universal tendencies.

Using an unmarked verb to report completed actions is grammaticized in some languages, such as the Niger-Congo languages of Yoruba and Igbo. In these languages, what is commonly called the "past" by Western grammarians is simply not marked. The reference of such unmarked verbs is to not always past time, but rather to completed aspect. This construction seems to express an attitude toward action: the most obvious feature of an action verb is that the action took place, happened, was observed; and in expressing action this feature need not be marked. For other forms of noncompleted or unrealized action an additional marking must be placed on the verb to express the less obvious condition. Welmers (1973) calls this African verb structure "factative," perhaps because the unmarked verb reports facts—action that took place. Although the systems differ in other ways, this is the same solution which Tomiko arrived at for reporting events. This system may be related to others occurring cross-linguistically, to some strategy concerning narratives, and ultimately to an extra-linguistic explanation, such as one based on perception. I look at the existence of "factative" languages as support for the viewpoint that Tomiko's tense-aspect system is a unique but far from arbitrary creation, at the very least. At most, it is a system through which we can refine our understanding of the general properties of language.

Let me illustrate with another example. All languages, it seems, have aspectual designations, though not all languages have tense distinctions. This suggests that aspect is somehow primary to tense in terms of grammaticizing temporal systems, which makes sense when we consider how easily time reference may be expressed with adverbials or other lexical items. In analyzing data from learners who have stopped acquiring English at a very rudimentary level, in terms of the target, I found that tense was never grammaticized— instead, the first distinction was aspectual. Typically, one broad distinction was made between completed and noncompleted action. If these findings are at all generalizable, they will support the claim that aspect is universally primary over tense.

At this point I must say that the discussion of the effect of universals on second language acquisition is very speculative for me; however, it is reasonable to assume that we can use universals—be they expressed as structures, tendencies, strategies, or so on—to aid in the task of understanding inter-language, and that we can use data from second language speakers as evidence in refining knowledge of universals.

In presenting the data in this way, I do not ignore the role of input: Tomiko shaped her interlanguage in the presence of spoken English, probably through a long process of hypothesis testing. Also, though the donations of her native Japanese are not so obvious, transfer on the level of category cannot be ruled out. The system was formed with sets of limitations which were both language-universal and language-specific, but the system was uniquely formed.

From the perspective of this single case study, it is not possible to show how prevalent the process is of regularizing unique grammatical relations to an internal norm. But if we consider the ways in which second languages are learned throughout the world, we must agree that contact learning is the usual case. Futhermore, most contact learning falls well short of mastery, and fossilization is probably a very common occurrence. How the resulting internalized systems are organized is of great interest in addressing the questions of input and transfer in acquisition, and in determining the role of universals in the acquisition process.

NOTES

1. The past expressions which show habituality are not neatly distinguished from those which do not. There are some instances where USETA appears in habitual contexts, as above. However, USETA may also come up when the context calls for a completive form, as with the adverbial in *I useta go with Bob for about four year*. It is difficult to say whether the marking is meant to relegate the information into the background, but the analysis presented here would say that it does. USETA may also be seem as a way to render a stative verb other than *be* into the past: *she useta have a nice house*. This would fit the claim that statives must be tensed. USETA, then, is clearly a background device, but it is not so clear that its meaning is "habitual."

References

Adjémian, Christian. 1976. On the nature of interlanguage systems. *Language Learning* 26:297–320.

Adjémian, Christian. 1982. La spécificité de l'Interlangue et l'idéalisation des langue secondes. In *Grammaire Transformationelle: Théorie et Méthodologies*, J. Guéron and T. Sowley (eds.), Université de Paris VIII.

Adjémian, C., and J. Liceras. In progress. *That* trace configurations and nonnative language acquisition. University of Ottawa.

Allen, C. 1980. Movement and deletion in Old English. *Linguistic Inquiry* 11:261–323.

Andersen, Roger. 1978. An implicational model for second language research. *Language Learning* 28:221–283.

Arditty, J., and C. Perdue. 1979. Variabilité et connaissances en langue étrangère. *Encrages*. Université de Paris VIII—Vincennes.

Bailey, N., C. Madden, and S. Krashen. 1974. Is there a "natural sequence" in adult second language learning? *Language Learning* 24:235–243. Reprinted in E. M. Hatch (ed.), *Second Language Acquisition*. Rowley, Mass.: Newbury House, 1978.

Baker, C. L. 1978. *Introduction to Generative-Transformational Syntax*. Englewood Cliffs, N.J.: Prentice-Hall.

Baker, C. L. 1979a. Remarks on complementizers, filters, and learnability. Ms., University of Texas, Austin.

Baker, C. L. 1979b. Syntactic theory and the projection problem. *Linguistic Inquiry* 10:533–581.

Beebe, L. 1980. Sociolinguistic variation and style shifting in second language acquisition. *Language Learning* 30:433–447.

Bialystok, E. 1981. The role of linguistic knowledge in second language use. *Studies in Second Language Acquisition* 4:31–45.

Bloom, L., P. Lightbown, and L. Hood. 1978. Pronominal-nominal variation in child language. In *Language Development*, Lois Bloom (ed.), New York: John Wiley & Sons, Inc.

Bransford, John D. 1979. *Human cognition*. Belmont, Calif.: Wadsworth.

Brown, Roger. 1973. *A First Language: The Early Stages*. Cambridge: Harvard University Press.

Carroll, John B. 1964. *Language and Thought*. Englewood Cliffs, N.J.: Prentice-Hall.

Carroll, J. M., T. G. Bever, and C. R. Pollack. 1981. The non-uniqueness of linguistics intuitions. *Language* 57:368–382.

Chomsky, N. 1964. On the notion of "rule of grammar." In *The Structure of Language*, J. Fodor and J. Katz (eds.), Englewood Cliffs, N.J.: Prentice-Hall.

Chomsky, N. 1965. *Aspects of the Theory of Syntax*, Cambridge, Mass.: MIT Press.

Chomsky, N. 1966. *Cartesian Linguistics*. New York: Harper and Row.

Chomsky, N. 1980. *Rules and Representation*. New York: Columbia University Press.

Chomsky, N. 1981a. *Lectures on Government and Binding*. Dordrecht: Foris Publications.

Chomsky, N. 1981b. Principles and parameters in syntactic theory. In *Explanations in Linguistics*, N. Hornstein and D. Lightfoot (eds.), London: Longman.

Chomsky, N. 1981c. Markedness and core grammar. In *Theory of Markedness in Generative Grammar,* A. Belletti, L. Brandi and L. Rizzi (eds.). Pisa: Scuola Normale Superiore.

Chomsky, N. 1982. *Some Concepts and Consequences of the Theory of Government and Binding.* Cambridge, Mass.: MIT Press.

Chomsky, N., and H. Lasnik. 1977. Filters and control. *Linguistic Inquiry* 8:425–504.

Cohen, Andrew, and Carol Hosenfeld. 1981. Some uses of mentalistic data in second language research. *Language Learning* 31:285–314.

Collins, Allan M., and M. Ross Quillian. 1972. Experiments in semantic memory and language comprehension. In *Cognition in Learning and Memory*, Lee W. Greeg (ed.), New York: John Wiley & Sons, Inc.

Corder, S. P. 1967. The significance of learners' errors. *International Review of Applied Linguistics* 5:161–170.

Corder, S. P. 1973. The elicitation of interlanguage. In *Errata: Papers in Error Analysis*, Jan Svartvik (ed.), Lund: CWK Gleerup.

de Villiers, J., and P. de Villiers. 1973. A Cross Sectional Study of the Development of Grammatical Morphemes in Child Speech. *Journal of Psycholinguistic Research* 2:267–278.

Dickerson, L. 1974. Internal and external patterning of phonological variability in the speech of Japanese learners of English. Ph.D dissertation, University of Illinois.

Dickerson, L., and W. Dickerson. 1977. Interlanguage phonology: current research and future directions in the notions of simplification, interlanguages and pidgins: In *Actes du 5eme Colloque de Linguistique Appliqué de Neufchatel*, S. P. Corder and E. Roulet (eds.).

Dore, J. 1978. Requestive systems in nursery school conversations: analysis of talk in its social context. In *Recent Advances in the Psychology of Language: Language Development and Mother-Child Interaction*, R. Campbell and P. Smith (eds.), New York: Plenum Press.

Dulay, H., and M. Burt. 1972. Goofing: An indicator of children's second language learning strategies. *Language Learning* 22:235–252.

Dulay, H. and M. Burt. 1973. Should we teach children syntax? *Language Learning* 23:245–258.

Dulay, H. and M. Burt. 1974. A new perspective on the creative constructive process in child second language acquisition. *Language Learning* 24:253–278.

Dulay, H. and M. Burt. 1975. A new approach to discovering universal strategies of child second language acquisition. In *Developmental Psycholinguistics: Theory and Applications*, D. P. Dato (ed.), Georgetown: Georgetown University Press.

Dulay, H. and M. Burt. 1978. Some remarks on creativity in language acquisition. In *Second Language Acquisition Research*, William C. Ritchie (ed.), New York: Academic Press.

Ervin-Tripp, S. 1974. Is second language learning like the first? *TESOL Quarterly* 8:111–127.

Faerch, Claus, and Gabriele Kasper. 1980. Processes and strategies in foreign language learning and communication. *Interlanguage Studies Bulletin* 5:47–119.

Fairbanks, K. 1982. Variability in Interlanguage. Masters qualifying paper, ESL Program: University of Minnesota.

Felix, S. 1980. The effect of formal instruction on second language acquisition. Paper presented at the Second Language Research Forum, Los Angeles, March 1980. Available: S. Felix, University of Passau, W. Germany.

Ferguson, C. and C. DeBose. 1977. Simplified registers, broken language and pidginization. In *Pidgin and Creole Linguistics*, A. Valdman (ed.), Bloomington, Ind.: Indiana University Press.

Filmore, C. 1965. *The Indirect Object Construction in English and the Ordering of Transformations.* The Hague: Mouton.

Fischer, S. 1971. The acquisition of verb-particle and dative constructions. Ph.D. Dissertation, MIT.

Fischer, S. 1976. Child language as a predictor of language change. *Working Papers in Linguistics* 8:71–104. University of Hawaii.

Flynn, A. 1981. Effects of the reversal of principal branching direction (from L1 to L2) in L2 acquisition. In *Cornell University Working Papers in Linguistics*, 2, W. Harbert and J. Herschensohn (eds.), Ithaca, N.Y.: Cornell University.

Flynn, A. 1983. A study of the effects of principle branching direction in second language acquisition: the generalization of a parameter of universal grammar from first to second language acquisition. Ph.D. Dissertation, Cornell University.

Fodor, J. D. 1978. Parsing strategies and constraints on transformations. *Linguistic Inquiry* 9:427–473.

Fodor, J. D. 1980. On the impossibility of acquiring more powerful structures. In *Language and Learning: The Debate between Jean Piaget and Noam Chomsky*, M. Piattelli-Palmarini (ed.), Cambridge, Mass.: Harvard University Press.

Fodor, J. D., and L. Frazier. 1980. Is the human sentence parsing mechanism an ATN? *Cognition* 8:417–459.

Foley, B. and H. Pomann. 1981. *Lifelines*. New York: Regents.

Gardner, R. C., and W. E. Lambert. 1972. *Attitudes and Motivation in Second Language Learning*, Rowley, Mass.: Newbury House.

Gass, S. 1979. Language transfer and universal grammatical relations. *Language Learning* 29:327–344.

Gass, S. 1980. An investigation of syntactic transfer in adult second language learners. In *Issues in Second Language Research*, S. Krashen and R. Scarcella (eds.), Rowley, Mass.: Newbury House.

Givón, Talmy. 1982. Tense-aspect-modality: The creole prototype and beyond. In *Tense and Aspect: Between Semantics and Pragmatics*, Paul Hopper (ed.), Amsterdam: J. Benjamin.

Goldsmith, J. 1979. Meaning and mechanism in grammar. In *Harvard Studies in Syntax and Semantics III*, S. Kuno (ed.). Cambridge, Mass.: Department of Linguistics, Harvard University.

Grice, H. P. 1975. Logic and conversation. In *Syntax and Semantics: Speech Acts*, P. Cole and J. Morgan (eds.), New York: Academic Press.

Hankamer, J. 1973. Unacceptable ambiguity. *Linguistic Inquiry* 4:17–68.

Hatch, Evelyn. 1975. Second language learning—universals? *Working Papers in Bilingualism* 3:1–18.

Hopper, Paul. 1979. Aspect and foregrounding in discourse. In *Syntax and Semantics: Discourse and Syntax*, Talmy Givón (ed.), New York: Academic Press.

Hornstein, N., and A. Weinberg. 1981. Case theory and preposition stranding. *Linguistic Inquiry* 12:55–92.

Huebner, Thom. 1979. Order of acquisition vs. dynamic paradigm: a comparison of method in interlanguage research. *TESOL Quarterly*, 13:21–28.

Hyltenstam, K. 1977. Implicational patterns in interlanguage syntax variation. *Language Learning* 27:383–411.

Hyltenstam, K. 1978. Variability in interlanguage syntax. *Phonetics Laboratory Working Papers* no. 18, Department of General Linguistics, Lund University, Sweden, 1–79.

Ioup, G., and A. Kruse. 1977. Interference vs. structural complexity as a predictor of second language relative clause acquisition. *Proceedings of the Second Language Acquisition Forum*. Los Angeles: UCLA.

Jackendoff, R. S., and P. Culicover. 1971. A reconsideration of dative movements. *Foundations of Language* 7:397–412.

Johansson, F. 1973. Immigrant Swedish phonology: a study in multiple contact analysis. Lund, Sweden: CWK Gleerup.

Kayne, R. S. 1976. French relative "que." *Current Studies in Romance Linguistics*. M. Lujan and F. Hensey (eds.), Washington, D.C.: Georgetown University Press.

Keenan, E. O., 1974. Conversational competence in children. *Journal of Child Language* 1:163–184.

Koster, J. 1978. *Locality Principles in Syntax*. Dordrecht: Foris Publications.

Krashen, S. 1976. Formal and informal linguistics environments in language learning and language acquisition. *TESOL Quarterly* 10:157–168.

Krashen, S. 1977. The monitor model for adult second language acquisition. In *Viewpoints on English as a Second Language*, M. Burt, H. Dulay and M. Finocchiaro (eds.), New York: Regents.

Krashen, S. 1978. The monitor model for second language acquisition. In *Second Language Acquisition and Foreign Language Teaching*. Rosario C. Gringas (ed.), Arlington: Center for Applied Linguistics.

Krashen, S. 1981. *Second Language Acquisition and Learning*. New York: Pergamon.

Krashen, S. and T. D. Terrell, 1983. *The Natural Approach,* San Francisco: The Alemany Press.

Krashen, S., C. Madden, and N. Bailey. 1975. Theoretical aspects of grammatical sequencing. In *On TESOL '75*, Marina Burt and Heidi Dulay (eds.), Washington: TESOL.

Kuroda, S-Y. 1968. Review of Fillmore (1965). *Language* 44:374–378.

Labov, W. 1969. The study of language in its social context. *Studium Generale* 23:30–87.

Lado, R. 1957. *Linguistics Across Cultures: Applied Linguistics for Teachers*. Ann Arbor: University of Michigan Press.

Langendoen, D. T., N. Kalish-Landon, and J. Dore. 1973. Dative questions: A study in the relation of acceptability to grammaticality of an English sentence type. *Cognition* 2:451–478.

Larsen-Freeman, D. 1975. The acquisition of grammatical morphemes by adult ESL students. *TESOL Quarterly* 9:409–430.

Larsen-Freeman, D. 1976. An explanation for the morpheme accuracy order of learners of English as a L2. *Language Learning* 26:125–135.

Lenneberg, Eric H. 1967. *Biological Foundations of Language*. New York: John Wiley & Sons, Inc.

Liceras, J. 1981. Markedness and permeability in interlanguage systems. *Working Papers in Linguistics*, Vol. 2. University of Toronto.

Liceras, J. 1983. Markedness, contrastive analysis and the acquisition of Spanish. Ph.D. Thesis, University of Toronto.

LoCoco, V. 1976. A comparison of three methods for data collection of second language data. *Working Papers in Bilingualism* 8:59–86.

Lust, B. 1981. Constraint on anaphora in early child language: A prediction for a universal. In Tavakolian (1981a).

Lust, B. 1983. On the notion "Principal branching direction": A parameter of universal grammar. In *Studies in Generative Grammar and Language Acquisition,* Y. Otsu, H. van Riemsdijk, K. Inoue, A. Kamio and N. Kawasaki (eds.), Tokyo: Monbusho Grant for Scientific Research.

Lust, B., and Y-C. Chien. 1980. Acquisition of coordination in first language acquisition of Mandarin Chinese. Paper presented at the biannual LSA meeting, summer 1980. Albuquerque, N.M.

Lust. B., and H. Barazangi. Ms. The structure of coordination in first language acquisition of Syrian Arabic. Cornell University.

Lust, B., and C. A. Mervis. 1980. Coordination in the natural speech of young children. *Journal of Child Language* 7:279–304.

Lust, B., K. Loveland, and K. Kornet. 1980. The development of anaphora in first language: syntactic and pragmatic constraints. *Linguistic Analysis* 6:217–249.

Lust, B., L. Solan, S. Flynn, C. Cross, and E. Schuetz. 1981. A comparison of constraints on the acquisition of null and pronominal anaphora in English. *Northeastern Linguistic Society*, vol. XI. Amherst: The University of Massachusetts.

Lust, B., and T. K. Wakayama. 1979. The structure of coordination in young children's acquisition of Japanese. In *Studies in First and Second Language Acquisition*, F. Eckman and A. Hastings (eds.), Rowley, Mass: Newbury House.

Lust, B., T. Wakayama, W. Synder, and M. Bergmann. In preparation. The acquisition of complex sentence structures in Japanese: a study of coordination in young Japanese children's natural speech.

Mazurkewich, I. 1981. Second language acquisition of the dative alternation and markedness: the best theory. Ph.D. Dissertation, Université de Montréal.

McCawley, James. 1978. Language universals in linguistic argumentation. *Linguistics in the Seventies: Directions and Prospects.* Braj B. Kachru (ed.), Urbana, Ill.: Department of Linguistics, University of Illinois.

Meyer, D. E., and R. W. Schvaneveldt. 1971. Facilitation in recognizing pairs of words: evidence of a dependence between retrieval operations. *Journal of Experimental Psychology* 90:227–234. (Cited in Bransford 1979.)

Meyer, D. E., and R. W. Schvaneveldt. 1976. Memory, memory structure and mental processes. In *The Structure of Human Memory*, C. N. Cofer (ed.), San Francisco: W. H. Freeman. (Discussed in Bransford 1979.)

Meyer, D. E., and R. W. Schvaneveldt, and M. G. Ruddy. 1974. Functions of graphemic and phonemic codes in usual word recognition. *Memory and Cognition* 2:309–321. (Discussed in Bransford 1979.)

Miller, George A. 1956. The magical number seven plus or minus two: Some limits on our capacity for processing information. *Psychological Review* 63:81–97.

Nelson, Katherine. 1979. Lecture on first language acquisition. Queens College, CUNY, March 1979.

Nemser, W. 1971. Approximative systems of foreign language learners. *IRAL* 9:115–123.

Oehrle, R. T. 1976. The grammatical status of the English dative alternation. Ph.D. Dissertation, MIT.

Otsu, Y. 1977. Dative questions and perceptual strategies. *Studies in English Linguistics* 5:163–173.

Paulston, C. B., and M. N. Bruder. 1976. *Teaching English as a Second Language.* Cambridge, Mass.: Winthrop Publishers.

Peck, S. 1978. Child-child discourse in second language acquisition. In *Second Language Acquisition: A Book of Readings*, E. M. Hatch (ed.), Rowley, Mass.: Newbury House.

Peters, Ann. 1977. Language learning strategies. *Language* 53:560–573.

Plann, Sandra. 1976. The Spanish immersion program: towards a native-like proficiency or a classroom dialect? Unpublished Master's Thesis, UCLA.

Read, C., and V. C. Hare. 1979. Children's interpretation of reflexive pronouns in English. In *Studies in First and Second-Language Acquisition,* F. Eckman and A. Hastings (eds.), Rowley, Mass.: Newbury House.

Richards, J. 1971. A non-contrastive approach to error analysis. *English Language Teaching* 25:204–219.

Richards, J. 1973. A non-contrastive approach to error analysis. In *Focus on the Learner: Pragmatic Perspectives for the Language Teacher*, In J. Oller and J. Richards (eds.), Rowley, Mass.: Newbury House.

Riemsdijk, H. van. 1978. *A Case Study in Syntactic Markedness: The Binding Nature of Preposition Phrases.* Lisse: The Peter de Ridder Press.

Rivero, M. L. 1980. That-Relatives and Deletion in Comp in Spanish. *Cahiers Linguistiques d'Ottawa*, Vol. 9. University of Ottawa.

Rivers, Wilga M. 1979. Learning a sixth language: an adult learner's diary. *Canadian Modern Language Review* 36:67–82.

Roeper, T., S. Lapointe, J. Bing, and S. Tavakolian. 1981. A lexical approach to language acquisition. In Tavakolian (1981).

Rosansky, Ellen. 1976. Methods and morphemes in L2 acquisition research. *Language Learning* 26:409–424.

Rosenblum, D., and M. Dorman. 1978. Hemispheric specialization for speech perception in language deficient kindergarten children. *Brain and Language* 6:378–389.

Ross, J. R. 1967. Constraints on variables in syntax. Ph.D. Dissertation, MIT.

Ross, J. R. 1968–1977. Goodbye *to whom*, hello *to who*. In *CLS Book of Squibbs Cumulative Index*, S. Fox, W. Beach, and S. Philosoph (eds.), Chicago, Ill.: University of Chicago.

Rubin, Joan. 1981. Study of cognitive processes in second language learning. *Applied Linguistics* 2:117–131.

Schachter, Jacqueline, and William Rutherford. 1979. Discourse function and language transfer. *Working Papers on Bilingualism* 19:1–12.

Schachter, J., A. Tyson, and F. Diffley. 1976. Learner intuitions of grammaticality. *Language Learning* 26:67–76.

Schmidt, M. 1980. Coordinate structures and language universals in interlanguage. *Language Learning* 30:397–416.

Schmidt, R. 1977. Sociolinguistic variation and language transfer in phonology. *Working Papers in Bilingualism* 12:79–95.

Schumann, J. H. 1976. Second language acquisition: the pidginization hypothesis. *Language Learning* 26:391–408.

Schumann, J. H. 1978. *The Pidginization Process: A Model for Second Language Acquisition.* Rowley, Mass.: Newbury House.

Seliger, H. 1982. Processing universals in second language acquisition. This volume.

Seliger, H. 1983. Learner interaction in the classroom and its effect on language acquisition. *Classroom Oriented Research in Second Language Acquisition*, In Herbert Seliger and Michael Long (eds.), Rowley, Mass.: Newbury House.

Selinker, L. 1972. Interlanguage. *IRAL* 10:209–231.

Selinker, Larry, and John Lamendella. 1979. The role of extrinsic feedback in interlanguage fossilization. *Language Learning* 29:363–376.

Sharwood-Smith, Michael. 1981. On interpreting language input. Paper presented at Lancaster Conference on Interpretive Strategies. Lancaster University, Lancaster, England, September 1981.

Slobin, D. I. 1973. Cognitive prerequisites for the development of grammar. In *Studies in Child Language Development,* Charles Ferguson and D. Slobin (eds.), New York: Holt, Rinehart and Winston.

Smith, D. 1978. Mirror images in Japanese and English. *Language* 54:78–122.

Spolsky, B. 1969. Attitudinal aspects of second language learning. *Language Learning* 19:272–283.

Stein, B. S. 1977. The effects of cue-target uniqueness on cued recall performance. *Memory and Cognition* 5:319–322. (Discussed in Bransford 1979.)

Stevick, E. W. 1982. *Teaching and Learning Languages.* New York: Cambridge University Press.

Stowell, T. A. 1981. Origins of phrase structure. Ph.D. Dissertation, MIT.

Stowell, T. A. 1982. NP-incorporation. Paper presented at the Canadian Linguistic Association Annual Meeting, Ottawa, 1982.

Tarone, E. 1979. Interlanguage as chameleon. *Language Learning* 29:181–191.

Tarone, E. 1980. Communication strategies, foreigner talk, and repair in interlanguage. *Language Learning* 30:417–432.

Tarone, E. 1982. Systematicity and attention in interlanguage. *Language Learning* 32:69–84.

Tarone, E., U. Frauenfelder, and L. Selinker. 1976. Systematicity/variability and stability/instability in interlanguage systems. In *Papers in Second Language Acquisition (Language Learning* Special Issue no. 4), H. Douglas Brown (ed.).

Tavakolian, S. (ed.) 1981. *Language Acquisition and Linguistic Theory.* Cambridge, Mass.: MIT Press.

Taylor, B. 1974. Toward a theory of language acquisition. *Language Learning* 24:23–36.

Terrell, Tracy. 1978. Adaptación de los estudios dialectales. In *Corrientes actuales en la dialectología del Caribe hispánico.* Humberto López-Morales (ed.), Puerto Rico: Editorial Universitario.

VanPatten, Bill. 1980. The acquisition of the copula and the preterit tense in two first year students of Spanish. Unpublished Master's Thesis, The University of Texas at Austin.

Vinet, M-T. 1979. Dialect variation and a restrictive theory of grammar: a student of intransitive prepositions in a variety of French. *Montreal Working Papers in Linguistics* 13:107–125.

Wagner-Gough, Judy, and Evelyn Hatch. 1975. The importance of input data in L2 acquisition. *Language Learning* 25:297–308.

Wanner, E., and M. Maratsos. 1978. An ATN approach to comprehension. In *Linguistic Theory and Psychological Reality*, M. Halle, J. Bresnan, and G. Miller (eds.), Cambridge, Mass.: MIT Press.

Welmers, William. 1973. *African Language Structures*. Berkeley: University of California Press.

White, L. 1980. Grammatical Theory and Language Acquisition. Bloomington, Ind.: Indiana University Linguistics Club.

Wode, H. 1978. Developmental sequences in naturalistic L2 acquisition. In *Second Language Acquisition*, Evelyn Hatch (ed.), Rowley, Mass.: Newbury House.

Wong-Fillmore, L. 1976. The second time around: cognitive and social strategies in second language acquisition. Ph.D. Dissertation, Stanford University.

Woods, William A. 1980. Multiple theory formation in speech and reading. In *Theoretical Issues in Reading Comprehension*, R. J. Spiro, B. C. Bruce, and W. F. Brewer (eds.), Hillsdale, N.J.: Lawrence Erlbaum Associates.